Teacher's

Authors

Dr. Nancy L. Roser

Professor, Language and Literacy Studies

The University of Texas

College of Education

Austin, TX

Dr. Jean Wallace Gillet

Reading Specialist

Charlottesville Public Schools

Charlottesville, VA

Program Consultant

Marilyn Jager Adams

Harvard University

Cambridge, MA

**SRA
McGraw-Hill**

Columbus, Ohio

A Division of The McGraw·Hill Companies

Cover Photos: tl STUDIOHIO, **tr** Aaron Haupt, **bc** Paul Chauncey/The Stock Market,
br George Schiavone/The Stock Market.

Illustrations: Steve McInturff

SRA/McGraw-Hill

*A Division of The **McGraw·Hill** Companies*

Copyright © 1999 by SRA/McGraw-Hill.

Send all inquiries to:
SRA/McGraw-Hill
250 Old Wilson Bridge Road
Suite 310
Worthington, Ohio 43085

Printed in the United States of America.

ISBN 0-02-674917-3

 3 4 5 6 7 8 9 DBH 04 03 02 01 00 99

TABLE OF CONTENTS

TABLE OF CONTENTS

TABLE OF CONTENTS

Name _____ **Date** _____

Level 2, Lesson 1

The /a/ Sound

Fold the paper in half. Use the blanks to write each word as it is read to you. Then, unfold the paper and correct any mistakes. Practice these words.

1. _____	1. *lap*
2. _____	2. *hat*
3. _____	3. *man*
4. _____	4. *ram*
5. _____	5. *bad*
6. _____	6. *map*
7. _____	7. *pat*
8. _____	8. *mad*
9. _____	9. *jam*
10. _____	10. *gas*

The /a/ Sound

Name _____ **Date** _____

Level 2, Lesson 1
The /a/ Sound

Follow along as your teacher reads each sentence. Write the Core Words in the correct blanks. Check your spelling.

1. I sat on Grandma's _____ and looked at

   a _____ of our town.

2. You can _____ your head or put your

   _____ on it.

3. That _____ likes bread with _____.

4. An angry goat can be called a _____

   _____!

5. It's too _____ your car ran out of

   _____.

Name _____ **Date** _____

Level 2, Lesson 1
The /a/ Sound

Words in the dictionary are in ABC order.

a b c d e f g h i j k l m n o p q r s t u v w x y z

CORE WORDS

lap
hat
man
ram
bad
map
pat
mad
jam
gas

Write the letter that comes before each letter.

1. d _____   2. g _____   3. b _____

Write the letter that comes after each letter.

4. m _____   5. r _____   6. v _____

Write the letters in ABC order.

7. fdce _____

8. qnpo _____

9. mlon _____

10. kihj _____

Name _____ **Date** _____

Level 2, Lesson 1
The /a/ Sound
PUZZLE

Find the Core Words in this word search.
Use the Core Word list to help you.

X	W	F	N	P	Q	E	G
P	B	I	R	A	K	Z	A
N	A	H	A	T	U	V	S
D	V	S	B	R	A	M	F
R	S	J	A	M	B	D	I
P	M	A	D	A	B	B	I
L	A	P	N	P	C	I	A
S	N	O	V	A	L	M	H

CORE WORDS

lap
hat
man
ram
bad
map
pat
mad
jam
gas

Name _____ Date _____

Level 2, Lesson 1

The /a/ Sound

SUPER SPELLER WORDS

almond

jacket

jackal

PHONETIC PATTERNS

Write each Super Speller Word and circle the /a/ sound.

1. _____

2. _____

3. _____

CONTEXT CLUES

Write a Super Speller Word to complete each sentence.

4. I put on my red _____.

5. Will you eat an _____?

6. John saw a _____ at the zoo.

Name _____ **Date** _____

Level 2, Lesson 1

The /a/ Sound

CROSS-CURRICULAR WORDS

valley
tax
cactus

LETTER CLUES

Write the missing letters to complete the
Cross-Curricular Words.

1. _____ _____ _____ley

2. t_____x

3. _____ _____ _____tus

CLASSIFYING

Write the Cross-Curricular Word that fits each group.

4. plant, desert, prickly, _____

5. money, shopping, law, _____

6. land, low, near hills, _____

Name _____ **Date** _____

Level 2, Lesson 1

The /a/ Sound

Read the story. Find 8 misspellings and 4 other mistakes in the story. Use all 3 proofreading marks to correct the story. Write the misspelled words correctly on the lines.

Proofreading Marks					
⬭	misspelling	＝	make a capital letter	⊙	add a period

CORE WORDS

lap
hat
man
ram
bad
map
pat
mad
jam
gas

the man was in a jamm. He had to find his raam. "This is too bad," he said. "My car has no gass." He looked at the map in his lep it was a bad maap. The mun was sad He got med. Then he saw an animal chew a red haat. It was his ram, and he gave it a pat!

1. _____

2. _____

3. _____

4. _____

5. _____

6. _____

7. _____

8. _____

Name _____ **Date** _____

Level 2, Lesson 1
The /a/ Sound
CORE WORDS

lap	man	bad	pat	jam
hat	ram	map	mad	gas

Always capitalize:

1. the first word in every sentence.

2. names of people.

The first word in every sentence begins with a capital letter. Circle the word in each sentence that should begin with a capital letter. Write the word correctly on the lines. Then underline the Core Words.

1. the hat was too big. _____

2. pat the dog softly. _____

3. is there gas in the car? _____

4. david is the man to ask. _____

5. her baby sat on my lap. _____

Name _____   **Date** _____

Level 2, Lesson 2

The /i/ Sound

Fold the paper in half. Use the blanks to write each word as it is read to you. Then, unfold the paper and correct any mistakes. Practice these words.

1. _____	1. _____ *if*
2. _____	2. _____ *zip*
3. _____	3. _____ *mix*
4. _____	4. _____ *pin*
5. _____	5. _____ *milk*
6. _____	6. _____ *tip*
7. _____	7. _____ *his*
8. _____	8. _____ *fix*
9. _____	9. _____ *kiss*
10. _____	10. _____ *rip*

Name _____ **Date** _____

Level 2, Lesson 2

The /i/ Sound

Follow along as your teacher reads each sentence. Write the Core Words in the correct blanks. Check your spelling.

1. I will _____ the tail on the donkey

   _____ I can.

2. Does Pat know _____ _____

   code?

3. The baby gave Mommy a _____

   on the _____ of her nose!

4. We added _____ to the pancake

   _____.

5. Please help me _____ the _____

   in my shirt.

Name _____ Date _____

Level 2, Lesson 2

The /i/ Sound

Words in the dictionary are in ABC order.

a b c d e f g h i j k l m n o p q r s t u v w x y z

CORE WORDS

if
zip
mix
pin
milk
tip
his
fix
kiss
rip

Write the word in each group that would come first in ABC order.

rip   kiss   milk   rip   if   kiss
_____   _____
- - - - - - - - - - - -   - - - - - - - - - - - -

1. _____   3. _____

his   mix   pin   tip   zip   rip
_____   _____
- - - - - - - - - - - -   - - - - - - - - - - - -

2. _____   4. _____

Write the word in each group that would come last in ABC order.

fix   milk   kiss   pin   mix   tip
_____   _____
- - - - - - - - - - - -   - - - - - - - - - - - -

5. _____   7. _____

milk   pin   rip   rip   pin   zip
_____   _____
- - - - - - - - - - - -   - - - - - - - - - - - -

6. _____   8. _____

10 The /i/ Sound

Name _____ **Date** _____

Level 2, Lesson 2
The /i/ Sound
LETTER SCRAMBLE

Unscramble the underlined Core Word.

1. I have to <u>ixm</u> the batter in the bowl.

   _____

   - - - - - - - - - - - - - - - - - -

   _____

2. Raise your hand <u>fi</u> you want to go.

   _____

   - - - - - - - - - - - - - - - - - -

   _____

3. You need nails and a hammer to <u>xif</u>

   _____

   - - - - - - - - - - - - - - - - - -

   this. _____

4. Let's play <u>inP</u> the Tail on the Donkey!

   _____

   - - - - - - - - - - - - - - - - - -

5. How did you <u>rpi</u> your pants?

   _____

   - - - - - - - - - - - - - - - - - -

   _____

6. It looks like the glass might <u>tpi</u> over.

   _____

   - - - - - - - - - - - - - - - - - -

   _____

**CORE
WORDS**

if
zip
mix
pin
milk
tip
his
fix
kiss
rip

Name _____ Date _____

Level 2, Lesson 2
The /i/ Sound
SUPER SPELLER WORDS
mistakes   twig   discover

WORD SORT

Sort the Super Speller Words by the number of syllables each word has.

One Syllable

1. _____

Two Syllables

2. _____

Three Syllables

3. _____

WORD PARTS

Write the Super Speller Words that have these smaller words in them.

4. takes _____

5. wig _____

6. cover _____

Name _____ Date _____

Level 2, Lesson 2

The /i/ Sound

CROSS-CURRICULAR WORDS

sixty
inch
number strip

WORD BUILDING

Do these word problems. Then write the
Cross-Curricular Words or terms.

1. sixteen - een + y = _____

2. i + branch - bra = _____

3. number striped - ed = _____

WORD PARTS

Find smaller words in the Cross-Curricular Word below.
Write them on the lines.

4. strip

_____   _____

_____   _____

_____   _____

Name _____ Date _____

Level 2, Lesson 2

The /i/ Sound

Read the story. Find 8 misspellings and 4 other mistakes in the story. Use all 3 proofreading marks to correct the story. Write the misspelled words correctly on the lines.

Proofreading Marks					
⬭	misspelling	⹀	make a capital letter	⊙	add a period

CORE WORDS

if
zip
mix
pin
milk
tip
his
fix
kiss
rip

The boy had a rep in his coat. He tried to fex it with a pinn. The tep of the pin stuck in the zipper It would not zep.

he was late for school He had to mex his cereal with milk and eat it. Then he would kiis the baby and go to school. he will fix the coat after school, ef he can.

1. _____   5. _____

2. _____   6. _____

3. _____   7. _____

4. _____   8. _____

Name _____   **Date** _____

Level 2, Lesson 2

The /i/ Sound

CORE WORDS

if	mix	milk	his	kiss
zip	pin	tip	fix	rip

When a sentence:

1. tells something, use a period (.).

2. asks something, use a question mark (?).

3. shows a strong feeling, use an exclamation point (!).

Read the sentences. Put either a period, question mark, or exclamation point at the end. Then circle the Core Words.

1. His shoe is untied

2. If I run fast, I will win

3. Did you mix the soup

4. Don't tip that glass

5. Will the dog kiss the baby

6. Please don't buy milk

7. The dress will rip

8. I will fix the broken toys

Name _____ **Date** _____

Level 2, Lesson 3

The /o/ and /ô/ Sounds

Fold the paper in half. Use the blanks to write each word as it is read to you. Then unfold the paper and correct any mistakes. Practice these words.

1. _____	1.	*cot*
2. _____	2.	*fog*
3. _____	3.	*lot*
4. _____	4.	*log*
5. _____	5.	*got*
6. _____	6.	*dog*
7. _____	7.	*flop*
8. _____	8.	*jog*
9. _____	9.	*job*
10. _____	10.	*spot*

Name _____ **Date** _____

Level 2, Lesson 3
The /o/ and /ô/ Sounds

Follow along as your teacher reads each sentence. Write the Core Words in the correct blanks. Check your spelling.

1. Let's run and _____ around that hollow

   _____

   _____ .

2. My cat likes to _____ in her favorite

   _____

   _____ .

3. She likes rain and _____ a

   _____

   _____ .

4. Have you _____ a bed or a

   _____

   _____ for me?

5. My _____ is to walk the _____ .

Name _____ **Date** _____

Level 2, Lesson 3

The /o/ and /ô/ Sounds

Words in the dictionary are in ABC order.

a b c d e f g h i j k l m n o p q r s t u v w x y z

CORE WORDS

cot
fog
lot
log
got
dog
flop
jog
job
spot

Look at the first letter of each word. Write the word that comes first in ABC order.

1. got, cot, spot _____

2. log, job, flop _____

3. lot, spot, got _____

4. spot, job, dog _____

Look at the first letter in each word. Write the word that comes last in ABC order.

5. got, lot, jog _____

6. fog, log, spot _____

7. cot, fog, dog _____

Name _____ **Date** _____

Level 2, Lesson 3
The /o/ and /ô/ Sounds
CONTEXT CLUES

Use Core Words to complete these
tongue twisters.

1. Clumsy Carl crawled onto his

   _____

   _____ and quickly caught

   a cold.

   _____

2. The _____ and dinosaur
   danced until dawn and decided to
   drive to Denver.

3. Fanny Flame found five funny fish that

   _____

   could flip and _____

   forever. _____

4. Jolly Jim could _____ and
   jump and just drink jelly juice.

5. Fumbling Fred found his way through

   _____

   the _____ .

**CORE
WORDS**

cot
fog
lot
log
got
dog
flop
jog
job
spot

Name _____ **Date** _____

Level 2, Lesson 3
The /o/ and /ô/ Sounds
SUPER SPELLER WORDS

bottle   bonnet   snort

LETTER CLUES

Write the missing letters to complete each
Super Speller Word.

1. sn_____rt   3. b_____nnet

2. b_____ttle

RIDDLES

Write the Super Speller Word that best answers
each riddle.

4. I'm something you can wear on your head.

   _____

   What am I? _____

5. I'm a noise you make and I rhyme with the word *fort*.

   _____

   What am I? _____

6. I'm something from which you can drink.

   _____

   What am I? _____

Name _____ Date _____

Level 2, Lesson 3

The /o/ and /ô/ Sounds
CROSS-CURRICULAR WORDS

contracts   ostrich   rocket

LETTER CLUES

Write the missing letters to complete each
Cross-Curricular Word.

1. _____ _____ _____tracts   2. _____ _____trich

3. _____ _____ _____ _____et

WORD PARTS

4. Write the Cross-Curricular Word that has the word
   on in it.

   _____

5. Write the Cross-Curricular Word that has the word
   rich in it.

   _____

6. Write the Cross-Curricular Word that has the word
   rock in it.

   _____

Name _____ Date _____

Level 2, Lesson 3

The /o/ and /ô/ Sounds

Read the story. Find 8 misspellings and 4 other mistakes in the story. Use all 3 proofreading marks to correct the story. Write the misspelled words correctly on the lines.

Proofreading Marks					
⬭	misspelling	＝	make a capital letter	⊙	add a period

CORE WORDS

cot
fog
lot
log
got
dog
flop
jog
job
spot

I just gott a new job It is a lat of fun. my job is to walk a big doog. I take the dog to a quiet spet to run. Sometimes I jg while the dog runs. We run until we flop down under a tree! there is a logg under the tree I can sit on the log, but I wish I had a kot. I walk the dog in sun or rain or fog. My jop is fun!

1. _____

2. _____

3. _____

4. _____

5. _____

6. _____

7. _____

8. _____

Name _____ **Date** _____

Level 2, Lesson 3

The /o/ and /ô/ Sounds

CORE WORDS

cot	lot	got	flop	job
fog	log	dog	jog	spot

Use quotation marks before and after words a speaker says aloud.

Bob said, "I've read that book twice."

Put quotation marks around a speaker's exact words.
The first one is done for you. Then circle the Core Words.

1. The nurse said, "We need another (cot) here."

2. Alisha asked the nurse,   Should I stand on this spot?

3.   My dog will stay with you,   Clyde said to Alisha.

4. The nurse said,   You are all doing a fine job.

5. Alisha said,   I will have fun and flop on the cot.

Name _____ **Date** _____

Level 2, Lesson 4

The Final /k/ Sound

Fold the paper in half. Use the blanks to write each word as it read to you. Then, unfold the paper and correct any mistakes. Practice these words.

1. _____	1. *dock*
2. _____	2. *snack*
3. _____	3. *lock*
4. _____	4. *pack*
5. _____	5. *sick*
6. _____	6. *rock*
7. _____	7. *sack*
8. _____	8. *stick*
9. _____	9. *stack*
10. _____	10. *kick*

Name _____ **Date** _____

Level 2, Lesson 4

The Final /k/ Sound

Follow along as your teacher reads each
sentence. Write the Core Words in the
correct blanks. Check your spelling.

1. There is only one _____ of gum left in the

   _____.

2. Let's eat a _____ from your paper

   _____.

3. We _____ our boat at the _____.

4. I tried to _____ the ball, but I hit a hard

   _____ instead!

5. If I were not _____ I would eat a whole

   _____ of pancakes!

Name _____ Date _____

Level 2, Lesson 4

The Final /k/ Sound

Words in the dictionary are in ABC order.

a b c d e f g h i j k l m n o p q r s t u v w x y z

CORE WORDS

dock
snack
lock
pack
sick
rock
sack
stick
stack
kick

Look at the first letter in each group of words. Write each set of words in ABC order.

dock   snack   rock

1. _____ 3. _____

2. _____

rock   stick   kick

4. _____ 6. _____

5. _____

7. How do you find ABC order for the words *sack* and *stack*? Circle the letter next to the correct answer.

   a. After the first letter, look at the last letter.

   b. After the first letter, look at the second letter.

Name _____ Date _____

Level 2, Lesson 4

The Final /k/ Sound

CONTEXT CLUES

Write a Core Word to complete the title of each song. Begin each Core Word with a capital letter.

1. " _____ and Roll Is Here to Stay"

CORE WORDS

2. "Three Boats by the _____ "

3. "I Love My _____ Lunch"

dock
snack
lock
pack
sick
rock
sack
stick
stack
kick

4. "Here's a Key to _____ My Heart"

5. "_____ That Soccer Ball One More Time"

6. "I'll Nurse Your _____ Heart Until You're Well"

7. "A _____ of Logs and a Fire Burning"

Name _____ Date _____

Level 2, Lesson 4

The Final /k/ Sound

SUPER SPELLER WORDS

skunk

crock

cloak

PHONETIC PATTERNS

Put the Super Speller Words in ABC order and circle the final /k/ sound.

1. _____   3. _____

2. _____

DEFINITIONS

Write the Super Speller Word that fits each meaning.

4. An animal that can give off a bad smell: _____

5. A kind of pot or container: _____

6. A kind of loose coat: _____

Name _____ **Date** _____

Level 2, Lesson 4

The Final /k/ Sound

CROSS-CURRICULAR WORDS

tick   wick   track

PHONETIC PATTERNS

Write the Cross-Curricular Words in ABC order and circle the final /k/ sound in each.

_____   _____

1. _____   3. _____

_____

2. _____

RHYMING WORDS

Write the Cross-Curricular Word that best completes each rhyme.

4. I picked up a long, brown stick

_____

and saw a small, black _____.

5. When the bear went to attack,

_____

his foot made a big, deep _____.

6. She did not know which tool to pick

_____

to trim the candle's long, long _____.

Name _____ **Date** _____

Level 2, Lesson 4

The Final /k/ Sound

Read the story. Find 8 misspellings and 4 other mistakes in the story. Use all 3 proofreading marks to correct the story. Write the misspelled words correctly on the lines.

Proofreading Marks		
⬭ misspelling	＝ make a capital letter	⊙ add a period

CORE WORDS

dock
snack
lock
pack
sick
rock
sack
stick
stack
kick

Go for a walk to the top of the big rok. Take a snak of apples and some nuts You can pak the snack in a paper sack. put the sac in a backpack.

Bring a big stik to help you walk. Please loak the door before you leave Walk down to the lake and past the dok. If you see old cans, do not keck them. Stack them and put them in the trash later

1. _____ 5. _____

2. _____ 6. _____

3. _____ 7. _____

4. _____ 8. _____

Name _____ **Date** _____

Level 2, Lesson 4
The Final /k/ Sound

CORE WORDS

dock	lock	sick	sack	stack
snack	pack	rock	stick	kick

> **Put a comma:**
>
> 1. between the day and year in a date:
>   *October 19, 1997*
>
> 2. after a greeting: *Dear Michael,*
>
> 3. after a closing: *Your friend,*

Read the letter. Put commas where they belong. Then circle the Core Words.

October 25 1997

Dear Martha

   Today I went to the dock. It was my first day

out since I got sick. I found a box with a lock. It

wouldn't open. I threw a rock at it. I did kick it a

little. Then it opened. I found a stack of old

pictures.

Your good friend

Charles

Name _____ **Date** _____

Level 2, Lesson 5

The /nd/ and /st/ Sounds

Fold the paper in half. Use the blanks to write each word as it is read to you. Then, unfold the paper and correct any mistakes. Practice these words.

1. _____	1. *pond*
2. _____	2. *just*
3. _____	3. *band*
4. _____	4. *last*
5. _____	5. *sand*
6. _____	6. *list*
7. _____	7. *lost*
8. _____	8. *hand*
9. _____	9. *fast*
10. _____	10. *and*

Name _____ **Date** _____

Level 2, Lesson 5

The /nd/ and /st/ Sounds

Follow along as your teacher reads each sentence. Write the Core Words in the correct blanks. Check your spelling.

1. A _____ duck swam around and around

   the _____ .

2. Mom made a _____ of _____

   what we need for the picnic.

3. The _____ played music

   _____ the people danced.

4. He may be _____ , but he still came in

   _____ !

5. We covered Dad's _____ with some soft,

   warm _____ .

Name _____ Date _____

Level 2, Lesson 5

The /nd/ and /st/ Sounds

Words in the dictionary are in ABC order.

a b c d e f g h i j k l m n o p q r s t u v w x y z

CORE WORDS

pond
just
band
last
sand
list
lost
hand
fast
and

Look at the first letter in each group of words. Write each set of words in ABC order.

sand	band	last

1. _____   3. _____

2. _____

and	lost	just

4. _____   6. _____

5. _____

list	pond	fast	hand

7. _____   9. _____

8. _____   10. _____

Name _____ **Date** _____

Level 2, Lesson 5

The /nd/ and /st/ Sounds

PUZZLE

The Core Words are hidden in this puzzle. Look across and down to find them. Use the Core Word list to help you.

X	X	L	I	S	T	H
X	P	O	N	D	B	A
J	U	S	T	F	A	N
Z	X	T	S	A	N	D
A	A	N	D	S	D	J
N	L	A	S	T	Z	X

CORE WORDS

pond
just
band
last
sand
list
lost
hand
fast
and

Name _____ Date _____

Level 2, Lesson 5

The /nd/ and /st/ Sounds

SUPER SPELLER WORDS

strong

lend

stern

WORD SORT

Write the Super Speller Word or words that go with each spelling pattern.

st

1. _____

_____

2. _____

nd

3. _____

LETTER SCRAMBLE

Unscramble the letters to write the Super Speller Words.

4. gsrnto _____

5. nters _____

6. neld _____

Name _____ Date _____

Level 2, Lesson 5

The /nd/ and /st/ Sounds

CROSS-CURRICULAR WORDS

expands   gust   frond

SORT

Write the Cross-Curricular Word or Words that go with each spelling pattern.

/nd/	/st/
1. _____	3. _____
_____	
2. _____	

SYNONYMS

Write the Cross-Curricular Word that means nearly the same as the underlined words.

4. A balloon <u>gets bigger</u> _____ when you blow air into it.

5. A <u>sudden burst</u> _____ of wind blew that tree down.

6. The black bumps on the back of this <u>leaf of a fern</u> _____ are called spores.

Name _____ Date _____

Level 2, Lesson 5

The /nd/ and /st/ Sounds

Read the story. Find 8 misspellings and 4 other mistakes in the story. Use all 3 proofreading marks to correct the story. Write the misspelled words correctly on the lines.

Proofreading Marks					
⬯	misspelling	＝	make a capital letter	⊙	add a period

CORE WORDS

pond
just
band
last
sand
list
lost
hand
fast
and

My dog, Sandy, is lost. I saw her juss last night. we were near the pand. She was running in the sant. She runs fass, faster than i can.

I held out my han. "Here, Sandy," I called, endd she ran away as fast as she could. that was the lest time I saw her She has a white bande along her back. Have you seen her?

1. _____

2. _____

3. _____

4. _____

5. _____

6. _____

7. _____

8. _____

Name _____ Date _____

Level 2, Lesson 5

The /nd/ and /st/ Sounds

Core Words

pond	band	sand	lost	fast
just	last	list	hand	and

Use parentheses ( ) to give extra information.

The bugs (three of them) are part of the science fair.

We walked 5 miles (8 kilometers) on the trail.

Put parentheses around the extra information in each sentence. Then circle the Core Words.

1. I will listen to the new songs four of them the band recorded today.

2. My hand is 5 inches 12.5 centimeters across.

3. The pond is 1 mile 0.6 kilometers from the house.

4. I went to a scout meeting and an S.A.T. Students and Teachers meeting.

5. I mixed sand white and black sand in a pail.

6. Did you find that at the L.A.F. lost and found ?

7. The last gas station was 2 miles 3.2 kilometers away.

Name _____ **Date** _____

Level 2, Lesson 6

Review for Lessons 1-5

Fold the paper in half. Use the blanks to write each word as it is read to you. Then, unfold the paper and correct any mistakes. Practice these words.

1. _____	1.	*gas*
2. _____	2.	*milk*
3. _____	3.	*got*
4. _____	4.	*lock*
5. _____	5.	*sand*
6. _____	6.	*map*
7. _____	7.	*if*
8. _____	8.	*flop*
9. _____	9.	*stick*
10. _____	10.	*band*

Name _____ **Date** _____

Level 2, Lesson 6

Review for Lessons 1-5

Follow along as your teacher reads each sentence. Write the Core Words in the correct blanks. Check your spelling.

1. The _____ will play _____ you

   will listen.

2. A _____ tore the _____.

3. My dad put a _____ on the _____

   can.

4. Ann _____ some _____ for the cat.

5. Do not _____ onto the hot _____.

Name _____ Date _____

Level 2, Lesson 6

Review for Lessons 1-5

Read each answer. Fill in the space in the Answer Rows for the choice that has a spelling error. If there is no mistake, fill in the last answer space.

1. A mape
   B his
   C jog
   D hat
   E (No mistake)

2. F and
   G lap
   H zep
   J lot
   K (No mistake)

3. A pack
   B san
   C pat
   D fix
   E (No mistake)

4. F job
   G kick
   H pond
   J stak
   K (No mistake)

5. A mix
   B gott
   C sick
   D list
   E (No mistake)

6. F mad
   G kiss
   H spod
   J dock
   K (No mistake)

7. A jost
   B man
   C milk
   D log
   E (No mistake)

8. F rock
   G lost
   H jam
   J rip
   K (No mistake)

ANSWER ROWS 1. Ⓐ Ⓑ Ⓒ Ⓓ Ⓔ 3. Ⓐ Ⓑ Ⓒ Ⓓ Ⓔ 5. Ⓐ Ⓑ Ⓒ Ⓓ Ⓔ 7. Ⓐ Ⓑ Ⓒ Ⓓ Ⓔ
             2. Ⓕ Ⓖ Ⓗ Ⓙ Ⓚ 4. Ⓕ Ⓖ Ⓗ Ⓙ Ⓚ 6. Ⓕ Ⓖ Ⓗ Ⓙ Ⓚ 8. Ⓕ Ⓖ Ⓗ Ⓙ Ⓚ

Name _____ **Date** _____

Level 2, Lesson 6

Review for Lessons 1-5

School Then and Now

Talk to an older family member or a friend. Find out what school was like when that person was your age. Ask what subjects he or she studied. Ask about classroom tools or school sports. Then, write a paper, telling about school then and now. Use as many Core Words as you can.

Follow these steps:

1. Begin by telling what you are writing about. Name the person you have talked to.

2. Next, tell about school then and now.

3. End by explaining what you learned.

Remember...

• Take some time to plan.

• Write down any ideas you have on scrap paper.

• Write your paper.

• Look over your work. Check it for spelling and other mistakes. Fix any that you find.

Name _____ Date _____

Level 2, Lesson 6

Review for Lessons 1-5

Find the Core Word that is spelled correctly and fits best in the blank. Mark your answers in the Answer Rows.

1. Use only one _____ of butter.
   A pat   B patt   C pait   D padt

2. Did your grandma _____ you?
   F kis   G ciss   H kiss   J cis

3. We tried to bake a cake, but it was a _____.
   A fop   B flop   C flp   D flopp

4. I can _____ the ball over the house.
   F cik   G kik   H kikc   J kick

5. We had a test _____ week.
   A last   B las   C lasd   D lats

6. Spread the grape _____ on the hot bread.
   F gam   G jam   H jaim   J jamm

7. Can you _____ oil and water?
   A miks   B mics   C mex   D mix

8. After school, my _____ is to feed the dog.
   F chob   G jobb   H job   J jub

ANSWER ROWS   1. Ⓐ Ⓑ Ⓒ Ⓓ   3. Ⓐ Ⓑ Ⓒ Ⓓ   5. Ⓐ Ⓑ Ⓒ Ⓓ   7. Ⓐ Ⓑ Ⓒ Ⓓ
              2. Ⓕ Ⓖ Ⓗ Ⓙ   4. Ⓕ Ⓖ Ⓗ Ⓙ   6. Ⓕ Ⓖ Ⓗ Ⓙ   8. Ⓕ Ⓖ Ⓗ Ⓙ

Name _____ Date _____

Level 2, Lesson 6

Review for Lessons 1-5

Find the underlined part of each sentence that is misspelled. If all the words are correct, choose No mistake. Mark your answers in the Answer Rows.

1. The <u>man</u> will need a <u>hat</u> <u>iff</u> he goes outside.   <u>No mistake.</u>
       A   B C   D

2. We <u>got</u> <u>lost</u> in the thick <u>foug</u>.   <u>No mistake.</u>
       F G   H   J

3. I was <u>just</u> <u>sick</u>, <u>amd</u> now I am better.   <u>No mistake.</u>
          A B   C   D

4. Part of <u>his</u> <u>job</u> is to <u>jog</u> around the park.   <u>No mistake.</u>
           F G   H   J

5. Put the <u>stick</u> and the <u>logg</u> in this <u>spot</u>.   <u>No mistake.</u>
           A   B   C   D

6. My dad is <u>maed</u> because I spilled <u>milk</u> in his <u>lap</u>.   <u>No mistake.</u>
              F   G   H   J

7. I can <u>fix</u> this <u>ripp</u> in the <u>map</u> with tape.   <u>No mistake.</u>
       A   B   C   D

8. Dana slept on a <u>cot</u> by the <u>dok</u> <u>last</u> night.   <u>No mistake.</u>
              F   G H   J

ANSWER ROWS   1. Ⓐ Ⓑ Ⓒ Ⓓ   3. Ⓐ Ⓑ Ⓒ Ⓓ   5. Ⓐ Ⓑ Ⓒ Ⓓ   7. Ⓐ Ⓑ Ⓒ Ⓓ

                      2. Ⓕ Ⓖ Ⓗ Ⓙ   4. Ⓕ Ⓖ Ⓗ Ⓙ   6. Ⓕ Ⓖ Ⓗ Ⓙ   8. Ⓕ Ⓖ Ⓗ Ⓙ

Name _____ Date _____

Level 2, Lesson 6

Review for Lessons 1-5

Read each phrase. Choose the phrase in which the underlined word is not spelled correctly. Mark your answers in the Answer Rows.

1. A sit on your <u>laep</u>
   B lie on a <u>cot</u>
   C <u>if</u> you can
   D <u>dock</u> the boat

2. F small <u>pond</u>
   G <u>just</u> in time
   H eat a <u>snak</u>
   J <u>mix</u> up

3. A a tall <u>mann</u>
   B <u>lock</u> the door
   C an empty <u>lot</u>
   D <u>band</u> music

4. F feed the <u>ram</u>
   G a <u>bad</u> idea
   H the <u>last</u> cookie
   J drink <u>melk</u>

5. A <u>got</u> home
   B feel <u>sick</u>
   C big <u>dogg</u>
   D grains of <u>sand</u>

6. F <u>losd</u> her key
   G <u>list</u> of names
   H a hard <u>rock</u>
   J <u>tip</u> over

7. A <u>pat</u> her hand
   B <u>flop</u> over
   C <u>his</u> bike
   D a <u>sacc</u> lunch

8. F <u>mad</u> at you
   G throw the <u>stick</u>
   H <u>fiks</u> the tire
   J <u>kick</u> the can

ANSWER ROWS   1. Ⓐ Ⓑ Ⓒ Ⓓ   3. Ⓐ Ⓑ Ⓒ Ⓓ   5. Ⓐ Ⓑ Ⓒ Ⓓ   7. Ⓐ Ⓑ Ⓒ Ⓓ
              2. Ⓕ Ⓖ Ⓗ Ⓙ   4. Ⓕ Ⓖ Ⓗ Ⓙ   6. Ⓕ Ⓖ Ⓗ Ⓙ   8. Ⓕ Ⓖ Ⓗ Ⓙ

Name _____ Date _____

Level 2, Lesson 6

Review for Lessons 1-5

Read each phrase. Choose the phrase in which the underlined word is not spelled correctly for the way it is used in the phrase. Mark your answers in the Answer Rows.

1. A <u>rock</u> in the chair
   B a warm <u>hat</u>
   C a <u>stick</u> of books
   D <u>zip</u> your coat

2. F a thick <u>fog</u>
   G roll the <u>log</u>
   H <u>his</u> clothes
   J <u>pen</u> the tail

3. A <u>list</u> one in line
   B <u>kiss</u> on the cheek
   C <u>pack</u> the box
   D an important <u>job</u>

4. F <u>stack</u> of papers
   G <u>band</u> on the drum
   H road <u>map</u>
   J you <u>and</u> I

5. A pour the <u>milk</u>
   B spread the <u>jam</u>
   C <u>if</u> it rains
   D a soft <u>bad</u>

6. F a barking <u>dog</u>
   G fill the <u>sack</u>
   H <u>mad</u> puddle
   J a cold <u>pond</u>

7. A a <u>rip</u> apple
   B a <u>fast</u> car
   C the <u>last</u> song
   D <u>ram</u> the door

8. F pencil <u>tip</u>
   G one white <u>sick</u>
   H <u>spot</u> the bird
   J a morning <u>snack</u>

ANSWER ROWS
1. Ⓐ Ⓑ Ⓒ Ⓓ
2. Ⓕ Ⓖ Ⓗ Ⓙ
3. Ⓐ Ⓑ Ⓒ Ⓓ
4. Ⓕ Ⓖ Ⓗ Ⓙ
5. Ⓐ Ⓑ Ⓒ Ⓓ
6. Ⓕ Ⓖ Ⓗ Ⓙ
7. Ⓐ Ⓑ Ⓒ Ⓓ
8. Ⓕ Ⓖ Ⓗ Ⓙ

Name _____   **Date** _____

Level 2, Lesson 6

Review for Lessons 1-5

Use these Core Words from Lessons 1–5 to complete the puzzle.

Lesson 1
map
gas

Lesson 2
milk
if
fix
rip
mix

Lesson 3
fog
flop

Lesson 4
lock
rock
snack
stick

Lesson 5
sand
band

ACROSS

2. Mist
5. Blend together
6. Food between meals
7. I will help you _____ you help me.
9. Use a bucket and shovel with this.
10. Has its own key
11. Tear
12. Use this to find the location of things.

DOWN

1. Hard as a _____
2. Mend or repair
3. Fuel for car
4. Strike up the _____.
5. Something you drink
8. To flap loosely
9. Piece of thin wood

Name _____ **Date** _____

Level 2, Lesson 7

The /e/ Sound

Fold the paper in half. Use the blanks to write each word as it is read to you. Then, unfold the paper and correct any mistakes. Practice these words.

1. _____	1. _egg_
2. _____	2. _fed_
3. _____	3. _met_
4. _____	4. _yet_
5. _____	5. _went_
6. _____	6. _nest_
7. _____	7. _rest_
8. _____	8. _test_
9. _____	9. _bend_
10. _____	10. _send_

Name _____ Date _____

Level 2, Lesson 7

The /e/ Sound

Follow along as your teacher reads each
sentence. Write the Core Words in the
correct blanks. Check your spelling.

_____

1. We _____ out to breakfast and I

   had a scrambled _____.

2. The mother bird _____ her babies in the

   _____.

3. I never _____ anyone who could

   _____ over backward!

4. It is not _____ time for the spelling

   _____.

5. Please _____ the _____ of my

   class to the library.

Name _____ **Date** _____

Level 2, Lesson 7

The /e/ Sound

Words in the dictionary are in ABC order.

a b c d e f g h i j k l m n o p q r s t u v w x y z

CORE WORDS

egg
fed
met
yet
went
nest
rest
test
bend
send

Look at the first letter for each word. Write the words in ABC order.

1. _____

2. _____

3. _____

4. _____

5. _____

6. _____

7. _____

8. _____

9. _____

10. _____

Name _____ Date _____

Level 2, Lesson 7
The /e/ Sound
LETTER SCRAMBLE

Unscramble the underlined words.
Use the Core Word list to help you.

CORE WORDS

1. He <u>newt</u> for the paper.

   _____

   - - - - - - - - - - - - - - -

   _____

2. Please <u>sned</u> the book to me.

   _____

   - - - - - - - - - - - - - - -

   _____

3. My sister <u>efd</u> the hungry cat.

   _____

   - - - - - - - - - - - - - - -

   _____

4. Do not break the <u>geg</u>!

   _____

   - - - - - - - - - - - - - - -

   _____

5. He drew a picture of a bird's <u>snet</u>.

   _____

   - - - - - - - - - - - - - - -

   _____

6. Please <u>debn</u> your knees.

   _____

   - - - - - - - - - - - - - - -

   _____

egg
fed
met
yet
went
nest
rest
test
bend
send

52 The /e/ Sound

Name _____ **Date** _____

Level 2, Lesson 7

The /e/ Sound

SUPER SPELLER WORDS

helicopter
celery
rescue

SYLLABLES

Write each Super Speller Word and draw a line between the syllables. Use a dictionary to check your answers.

1. _____   3. _____

2. _____

CLASSIFYING

Write the Super Speller Word that fits each group.

4. carrots, beets, cabbage, _____

5. boat, car, airplane, _____

6. drown, save, _____

Name _____ **Date** _____

Level 2, Lesson 7

The /e/ Sound

CROSS-CURRICULAR WORDS

less than

twenty

set

LETTER CLUES

Write the missing letters to complete each Cross-Curricular Word or term.

1. s_____t

2. l_____ss than

3. tw_____nty

CONTEXT CLUES

Use Cross-Curricular Words to complete the story below.

My friend June and I each bought a chess

4. _____. My chess set cost 5. _____

dollars. June's chess set cost ten dollars. Her set cost

6. _____ mine.

Name _____ **Date** _____

Level 2, Lesson 7

The /e/ Sound

Read the story. Find 8 misspellings and 4 other mistakes in the story. Use all 3 proofreading marks to correct the story. Write the misspelled words correctly on the lines.

Proofreading Marks					
⬭	misspelling	＝	make a capital letter	⊙	add a period

Last week I wannt to a farm. The farmer mett me at the gate First I fad the hens and got the eggs. most eggs were white, but one eg was brown. It was in the smallest nast. I had to bend way down to get it. The farmer did a test on each egg Then we took a rast. It was not yat time for dinner. i wrote a letter about the farm to sind to my friend.

CORE WORDS

egg
fed
met
yet
went
nest
rest
test
bend
send

1. _____

2. _____

3. _____

4. _____

5. _____

6. _____

7. _____

8. _____

Name _____ Date _____

Level 2, Lesson 7
The /e/ Sound
CORE WORDS

egg	met	went	rest	bend
fed	yet	nest	test	send

Some words can be shortened. These words are called abbreviations:

Streets:	Street - St.	Avenue - Ave.
	Drive - Dr.	Road - Rd.
Titles:	Mister - Mr.	Mistress - Mrs.
	Doctor - Dr.	
Amounts:	pound(s) - lb(s)	inch(es) - in.
	minute(s) - min.	

Which word can be shortened? Write the abbreviation on the line. Then circle the Core Words.

1. Did you rest at 15 Barr Road? _____

2. Boil the egg for 1 minute. _____

3. They met on Jay Street. _____

4. Mister Ross will test the class. _____

Name _____ **Date** _____

Level 2, Lesson 8

The /u/ Sound

Fold the paper in half. Use the blanks to write each word as it is read to you. Then, unfold the paper and correct any mistakes. Practice these words.

1. _____   1. _____ us

2. _____   2. _____ mud

3. _____   3. _____ rub

4. _____   4. _____ rust

5. _____   5. _____ tug

6. _____   6. _____ luck

7. _____   7. _____ must

8. _____   8. _____ rug

9. _____   9. _____ shut

10. _____   10. _____ stuck

Name _____ Date _____

Level 2, Lesson 8

The /u/ Sound

Follow along as your teacher reads each sentence. Write the Core Words in the correct blanks. Check your spelling.

_____

1. Please _____ the door and help me

   clean the _____.

2. A scared little rabbit was _____ in the

   _____.

3. They gave a _____ on the nail that was

   covered with _____.

4. This present _____ be for

   _____!

5. I saw the boy _____ the lamp for good

   _____.

Name _____ **Date** _____

Level 2, Lesson 8

The /u/ Sound

Which part of the dictionary has the word you need? Think of the first letter of the word you want to find. Then use this chart.

CORE WORDS	abcdefghi look in the beginning	jklmnopq look in the middle	rstuvwxyz look in the end

us
mud
rub
rust
tug
luck
must
rug
shut
stuck

Where would you find these words? Write *beginning, middle,* or *end.*

1. us _____

2. mud _____

3. rub _____

4. tug _____

5. luck _____

6. must _____

7. rust _____

Name _____ Date _____

Level 2, Lesson 8
The /u/ Sound
PUZZLE

Use the Core Words to fill in the puzzle.

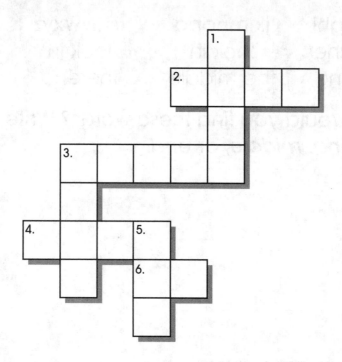

CORE WORDS

us
mud
rub
rust
tug
luck
must
rug
shut
stuck

Across

2. This is on old nails.

3. The door will not open; it is _____.

4. If you have to, you _____.

6. You and me

Down

1. Wish them good _____.

3. Close the door.

5. Pull on a rope.

Name _____ **Date** _____

Level 2, Lesson 8

The /u/ Sound

SUPER SPELLER WORDS

mustard
plumber
stuffy

LETTER CLUES

Write the missing letters to complete each Super Speller Word. Then write the word.

1. pl_____mber _____

2. m_____stard _____

3. st_____ffy _____

LETTER SCRAMBLE

Cross out the letters that don't belong to find each hidden Super Speller Word.

4. bpstuffylim

5. sykiplumberag

6. plmustardberry

Name _____ Date _____

Level 2, Lesson 8

The /u/ Sound

CROSS-CURRICULAR WORDS

function
subtraction
multiply

SYLLABLES

Write the Cross-Curricular Words. Circle the syllable that has the /u/ sound.

1. _____

2. _____

3. _____

WORD ENDINGS

Write the Cross-Curricular Words that have the same ending.

4. _____

5. _____

RELATED WORDS

Write the Cross-Curricular Word that has the same spelling pattern as each word.

6. subject _____

7. functional _____

8. multiple _____

PROOFREADING ACTIVITY

Name _____ **Date** _____

Level 2, Lesson 8

The /u/ Sound

Read the story. Find 8 misspellings and 4 other mistakes in the story. Use all 3 proofreading marks to correct the story. Write the misspelled words correctly on the lines.

Proofreading Marks					
⬭	misspelling	=	make a capital letter	⊙	add a period

Every Saturday I most wash the family car. I use a rag to rub away the mudd. I use another rag to rud the car until it shines. I will even rub russ away

my sister cleans the ruug in the car. If the car door seems stuk, we give it a tug. one tugg is all you need to open it. when we are done we shot the doors.

CORE WORDS

us
mud
rub
rust
tug
luck
must
rug
shut
stuck

1. _____

2. _____

3. _____

4. _____

5. _____

6. _____

7. _____

8. _____

Name _____ **Date** _____

Level 2, Lesson 8

The /u/ Sound

CORE WORDS

us	rub	tug	must	shut
mud	rust	luck	rug	stuck

Here are some rules about apostrophes:

1. When there is one owner, use 's.

2. When there is more than one owner, use s'.

Underline words that are missing apostrophes. Write the words with apostrophes on the lines. Then circle the Core Words.

1. Charlies "Help us!" sign was stuck to the shut door.

   _____

   -

   _____

2. He wanted his sisters friend to rub the rust off the car.

   _____

   -

   _____

   _____

   -

3. The friends name must be Tanya. _____

4. The rug was covered with mud from both girls shoes.

   _____

   -

   _____

Name _____ Date _____

Level 2, Lesson 9

Words with *gr, dr,* and *tr*

Fold the paper in half. Use the blanks to write each word as it is read to you. Then, unfold the paper and correct any mistakes. Practice these words.

1. _____	1. *grand*
2. _____	2. *drum*
3. _____	3. *tree*
4. _____	4. *drove*
5. _____	5. *grin*
6. _____	6. *truck*
7. _____	7. *drip*
8. _____	8. *trip*
9. _____	9. *drive*
10. _____	10. *gray*

Name _____ **Date** _____

Level 2, Lesson 9

Words with *gr*, *dr*, and *tr*

Follow along as your teacher reads each sentence. Write the Core Words in the correct blanks. Check your spelling.

1. We banged on a _____ that was made

   from a _____.

2. Does Kim's dad _____ a fire

   _____?

3. On our vacation _____ we saw a big

   _____ whale.

4. "I like to hear the rain _____," he said

   with a _____.

5. "Honk! Honk!" went the _____ old car as

   Grandma _____ along.

Name _____ **Date** _____

Level 2, Lesson 9

Words with *gr*, *dr*, and *tr*

Look at the first, second, third, and fourth
letters in each Core Word. Write the set of words in
ABC order.

**CORE
WORDS**

grand
drum
tree
drove
grin
truck
drip
trip
drive
gray

1. _____

2. _____

3. _____

4. _____

5. _____

6. _____

7. _____

8. _____

9. _____

10. _____

Name _____ Date _____

Level 2, Lesson 9

Words with *gr*, *dr*, and *tr*

PUZZLE

Find the Core Words in this word search.
Use the Core Word list to help you.

```
M   F   D   R   I   V   E   L
S   D   R   I   P   G   L   Q
T   R   U   C   K   R   O   O
R   O   M   T   B   I   X   V
E   V   G   R   A   N   D   W
E   E   Z   I   B   C   A   D
C   G   W   P   G   R   A   Y
```

CORE WORDS

grand
drum
tree
drove
grin
truck
drip
trip
drive
gray

Name _____ **Date** _____

Level 2, Lesson 9

Words with *gr, dr,* and *tr*

SUPER SPELLER WORDS

grasp
dreadful
trying

WORD SORT

Write the Super Speller Word that goes with each spelling pattern.

1. dr _____   3. tr _____

2. gr _____

DEFINITIONS

Write a definition for each Super Speller Word. Check your answers in a dictionary.

4. grasp: _____

5. dreadful: _____

6. trying: _____

Name _____ Date _____

Level 2, Lesson 9

Words with *gr*, *dr*, and *tr*

CROSS-CURRICULAR WORDS

graph   dragon   truth

WORD PARTS

Write the Cross-Curricular Word that belongs in each of the words below.

1. photo_____er   3. _____fly

2. _____fully

RHYMING WORDS

Write the Cross-Curricular Word that best completes the rhyme.

4. If you are a _____, you cannot fit in a wagon.

PLURALS

Write the Cross-Curricular Word that names one of each thing listed below.

5. dragons _____   7. graphs _____

6. truths _____

Name _____ Date _____

Level 2, Lesson 9

Words with *gr*, *dr*, and *tr*

Read the story. Find 8 misspellings and 4 other mistakes in the story. Use all 3 proofreading marks to correct the story. Write the misspelled words correctly on the lines.

Proofreading Marks					
⬭	misspelling	=	make a capital letter	⊙	add a period

"We are going to take a driv," called Mom

"where will we go on this tripp?" I asked.

"It is a secret," she said with a grinn.

We drov down the street, past the big tre. it was raining, and water began to dripp down the window.

Mom parked in front of a large grae house. I saw a woman playing a drum in the window We were going to hear a graned band!

CORE WORDS

grand
drum
tree
drove
grin
truck
drip
trip
drive
gray

1. _____   5. _____

2. _____   6. _____

3. _____   7. _____

4. _____   8. _____

Name _____ Date _____

Level 2, Lesson 9

Words with *gr*, *dr*, and *tr*

CORE WORDS

grand	tree	grin	drip	drive
drum	drove	truck	trip	gray

Some sentences:

1. make a statement and end with a (.).

2. ask questions and end with a (?).

3. show surprise and end with an (!).

4. give a command and end with a (.).

Punctuate these sentences. Then circle the Core Words.

1. Would you like to take a trip in that gray truck

2. We can drive by the grand old tree

3. What a big grin

4. Did she like the tree or our truck better

Write two sentences with the word *drip*. Make one a command and one a question.

5. command: _____

_____

_____

6. question: _____

Name _____ Date _____

Level 2, Lesson 10

Words with *gl*, *bl*, and *pl*

Fold the paper in half. Use the blanks to write each word as it is read to you. Then, unfold the paper and correct any mistakes. Practice these words.

1. _____	1. *plus*
2. _____	2. *glass*
3. _____	3. *blink*
4. _____	4. *plot*
5. _____	5. *glad*
6. _____	6. *blend*
7. _____	7. *plan*
8. _____	8. *block*
9. _____	9. *plum*
10. _____	10. *blast*

Name _____ Date _____

Level 2, Lesson 10

Words with *gl, bl,* and *pl*

Follow along as your teacher reads each
sentence. Write the Core Words in the
correct blanks. Check your spelling.

1. I am _____ I didn't hear that toy rocket

_____ off.

2. I had a _____ of milk and a _____.

3. We will _____ a science display

_____ a school play.

4. Did you _____ to make me

_____ so I couldn't see?

5. The colors on this building _____

_____ into each other.

Name _____ **Date** _____

Level 2, Lesson 10

Words with *gl*, *bl*, and *pl*

An entry word is the word you look up in the dictionary. A definition tells you what the word means. Many entry words have more than one meaning. Look up the word *plot* in your Speller Dictionary to answer the questions. Remember that entry words appear in ABC order.

CORE WORDS

plus
glass
blink
plot
glad
blend
plan
block
plum
blast

1. What is the entry word?

   _____

   -

   _____

2. What is the third meaning?

   _____

   -

   _____

3. What is the sentence given for the first meaning?

   _____

   -

   _____

   -

   _____

4. Which meaning is the main idea of a book?

   _____

   -

   _____

Name _____ Date _____

Level 2, Lesson 10

Words with *gl*, *bl*, and *pl*

PUZZLE

Use the Core Words to fill in the puzzle.

Across

2. Happy
3. Mix together
4. Something used to build
5. Something that can shatter
6. What happens in a story
7. Addition

Down

1. A way of doing something
3. You do this with your eyes
4. How a rocket starts
6. Sweet and sour fruit

CORE WORDS

plus
glass
blink
plot
glad
blend
plan
block
plum
blast

Name _____ **Date** _____

Level 2, Lesson 10
Words with *gl*, *bl*, and *pl*
SUPER SPELLER WORDS

blinker   glide   planetary

LETTER CLUES

Write the missing letters in the Super Speller Words.
Then write the words.

1. _____ _____ide   _____

2. _____ _____inker   _____

3. _____ _____anetary   _____

WORD BUILDING

Write the Super Speller Word that solves each word problem.

4. glad – ad + ide = _____

5. planet + ary = _____

6. blink + er = _____

Name _____ Date _____

Level 2, Lesson 10
Words with *gl*, *bl*, and *pl*
CROSS-CURRICULAR WORDS

plankton   blood   glade

PHONETIC PATTERNS

Write the Cross-Curricular Word that begins with **gl**.

1. _____

Write the Cross-Curricular Word that begins with **pl**.

2. _____

Write the Cross-Curricular Word that begins with **bl**.

3. _____

SYNONYMS

Write the Cross-Curricular Word that means nearly the same as the underlined words.

4. The fish ate the <u>tiny plants and animals</u> in the ocean.

_____

Name _____ **Date** _____

Level 2, Lesson 10

Words with *gl*, *bl*, and *pl*

Read the story. Find 8 misspellings and 4 other mistakes in the story. Use all 3 proofreading marks to correct the story. Write the misspelled words correctly on the lines.

Proofreading Marks					
⬭	misspelling	＝	make a capital letter	⊙	add a period

Ride your bicycle over to my blok. I have a good plaine. we can make a rocket and blats off. We will be in the sky in the blinc of an eye

We can look at the street under us through the window glas. Our rocket will go so fast, all the trees and houses will blent together

We can plat our trip on the space map. You will be glaad you came to my block

CORE WORDS

plus
glass
blink
plot
glad
blend
plan
block
plum
blast

1. _____

2. _____

3. _____

4. _____

5. _____

6. _____

7. _____

8. _____

Name _____ Date _____

Level 2, Lesson 10
Words with *gl*, *bl*, and *pl*
CORE WORDS

plus	blink	glad	plan	plum
glass	plot	blend	block	blast

Here are some facts about sentences:

1. A *complete sentence* has a subject and a verb.

2. An *incomplete sentence* is not a whole thought. It may not have a subject or a verb.

If the sentence is complete, put a ✓ in the box. If the sentence is incomplete, put an *x* in the box. Then circle the Core Words.

1. The block of glass. ☐

2. The plum tastes good. ☐

3. I blink. ☐

4. A blast happens in my story plot. ☐

5. Are glad. ☐

6. I blend the cake mix until. ☐

7. Two plus two makes four. ☐

8. We plan. ☐

Name _____ Date _____

Level 2, Lesson 11

Words with *sk, mp,* and *ng*

Fold the paper in half. Use the blanks to write each word as it is read to you. Then, unfold the paper and correct any mistakes. Practice these words .

1. _____
2. _____
3. _____
4. _____
5. _____
6. _____
7. _____
8. _____
9. _____
10. _____

1. *wing*
2. *dump*
3. *sting*
4. *mask*
5. *long*
6. *jump*
7. *desk*
8. *song*
9. *camp*
10. *ask*

Name _____ **Date** _____

Level 2, Lesson 11

Words with *sk, mp,* and *ng*

Follow along as your teacher reads each sentence. Write the Core Words in the correct blanks. Check your spelling.

1. The _____ I will sing is very

   _____ .

2. Please don't _____ trash around our

   _____ .

3. Don't touch a bee's _____, because

   the bee might _____ you.

4. Put your Halloween _____ in your

   _____ .

5. Did you _____ him to _____

   rope with us?

Name _____ **Date** _____

Level 2, Lesson 11

Words with *sk, mp,* and *ng*

Use this chart to help you look in the right part
of a dictionary to find words.

CORE WORDS	abcdefghi look in the beginning	jklmnopq look in the middle	rstuvwxyz look at the end

wing
dump
sting
mask
long
jump
desk
song
camp
ask

Write the first seven Core Words in the
correct part of the chart.

	Beginning	Middle	End
1.			
2.			
3.			
4.			
5.			
6.			
7.			

Name _____ Date _____

Level 2, Lesson 11

Words with *sk, mp,* and *ng*

RIDDLES

Write a Core Word to finish each sentence. Then use the letters in the boxes to make a word that answers the riddle.

1. The ____ ____ ☐ ____ truck will drop the soil.

2. Please ☐ ____ ____ me that question again.

3. Make sure the bee doesn't ☐ ____ ____ ____ you.

4. I sit at my ____ ____ ☐ to do my homework.

5. What do you use to look different?

____ ____ ____ ____

____ ____ ____ ____

CORE WORDS

wing
dump
sting
mask
long
jump
desk
song
camp
ask

Name _____ **Date** _____

Level 2, Lesson 11

Words with *sk, mp,* and *ng*

SUPER SPELLER WORDS

cask   lump   fling

WORD SORT

Sort the Super Speller Words by their endings.

_____

1. Write the word that ends with **sk**. _____

_____

2. Write the word that ends with **mp**. _____

_____

3. Write the word that ends with **ng**. _____

SYNONYMS

Write the Super Speller Word that means the same as each word below.

_____

4. throw: _____

_____

5. bump: _____

_____

6. barrel: _____

Name _____ **Date** _____

Level 2, Lesson 11

Words with *sk*, *mp*, and *ng*

CROSS-CURRICULAR WORDS

stump   ring   dusk

PHONETIC PATTERNS

1. Write the Cross-Curricular Word that has the same ending as the word *bump*.

   _____

   ----

2. Write the Cross-Curricular Word that has the same ending as the word *sting*.

   _____

   ----

3. Write the Cross-Curricular Word that has the same ending as the word *husk*.

   _____

RHYMING WORDS

Write the Cross-Curricular Word that best completes the rhyme.

4. There was a smell of musk

   _____

   ----

   in the air at _____.

Name _____ **Date** _____

Level 2, Lesson 11

Words with *sk, mp,* and *ng*

Read the story. Find 8 misspellings and 4 other mistakes in the story. Use all 3 proofreading marks to correct the story. Write the misspelled words correctly on the lines.

Proofreading Marks					
⬭	misspelling	＝	make a capital letter	⊙	add a period

get a funny masshk so no one will guess who you are. You could be a bee that does not steng.

Next, campe out near the door Hide behind a dessk. be careful not to dupp any books onto the floor.

Wait for a loge time. When people come, they will acks, "Who is it?" then you can junp out and sing a song. They will be surprised!

CORE WORDS

wing
dump
sting
mask
long
jump
desk
song
camp
ask

1. _____

2. _____

3. _____

4. _____

5. _____

6. _____

7. _____

8. _____

Name _____ Date _____

Level 2, Lesson 11

Words with *sk, mp,* and *ng*

CORE WORDS

wing	sting	long	desk	camp
dump	mask	jump	song	ask

> **Compound subjects tell about more than one subject. The word *and* joins the two subjects.**
>
> *Ants* and *worms crawl on the ground.*
>
> **Compound verbs tell about a subject that does more than one thing. The word *and* joins the two verbs.**
>
> *Children read* and *write in class.*

Draw a circle around two subjects and the word *and*.

1. The desks and masks are brown.

2. The dump and the camp have a sign in front of them.

Draw a circle around two verbs and the word *and*.

3. The bug will jump and sting a smaller bug.

4. Children read first and ask questions later.

Name _____ **Date** _____

Level 2, Lesson 12

Review for Lessons 7–11

Fold the paper in half. Use the blanks to write each word as it is read to you. Then, unfold the paper and correct any mistakes. Practice these words.

1. _____	1. *yet*
2. _____	2. *mud*
3. _____	3. *drive*
4. _____	4. *plus*
5. _____	5. *mask*
6. _____	6. *met*
7. _____	7. *shut*
8. _____	8. *grin*
9. _____	9. *blast*
10. _____	10. *sting*

Name _____ **Date** _____

Level 2, Lesson 12

Review for Lessons 7-11

Follow along as your teacher reads each
sentence. Write the Core Words in the correct
blanks. Check your spelling.

1. Before you put the car in _____ _____,

   _____

   _____ the door.

2. We have not _____ our new teacher

   _____

   _____.

3. No one can see your _____ behind that

   _____

   _____.

4. I have heard you should put _____ on a bee

   _____

   _____.

5. The noise from the _____ _____

   the surprise scared me.

Name _____ Date _____

Level 2, Lesson 12

Review for Lessons 7–11

Read each answer. Fill in the space in the Answer Rows for the choice that has a spelling error. If there is no mistake, fill in the last answer space.

1. A yiet
   B tug
   C truck
   D plan
   E (No mistake)

2. F song
   G bend
   H stuck
   J grand
   K (No mistake)

3. A glas
   B sting
   C went
   D luck
   E (No mistake)

4. F drip
   G block
   H canp
   J send
   K (No mistake)

5. A us
   B derum
   C blink
   D tree
   E (No mistake)

6. F nist
   G must
   H trip
   J plum
   K (No mistake)

7. A ask
   B egg
   C mud
   D masck
   E (No mistake)

8. F plot
   G long
   H rest
   J rug
   K (No mistake)

ANSWER ROWS 1. Ⓐ Ⓑ Ⓒ Ⓓ Ⓔ 3. Ⓐ Ⓑ Ⓒ Ⓓ Ⓔ 5. Ⓐ Ⓑ Ⓒ Ⓓ Ⓔ 7. Ⓐ Ⓑ Ⓒ Ⓓ Ⓔ
             2. Ⓕ Ⓖ Ⓗ Ⓙ Ⓚ 4. Ⓕ Ⓖ Ⓗ Ⓙ Ⓚ 6. Ⓕ Ⓖ Ⓗ Ⓙ Ⓚ 8. Ⓕ Ⓖ Ⓗ Ⓙ Ⓚ

Name _____ Date _____

Level 2, Lesson 12

Review for Lessons 7-11

Growth Watch

Choose a living thing that you have watched grow. This might be a tree near your home or a younger brother or sister. Write about the changes you have seen. Use as many Core Words as you can.

Follow these steps:

1. Begin by telling what you are writing about.

2. Then tell about the plant, animal, or person that you are writing about.

3. Tell how it has changed over months or years. Write the changes in the order they happened. Include lots of details.

4. End by telling what this living thing needs to grow.

Remember...

• Take some time to plan.

• Write down any ideas you have on scrap paper.

• Write your paper.

• Look over your work. Check it for spelling and other mistakes. Fix any that you find.

Name _____ **Date** _____

Level 2, Lesson 12

Review for Lessons 7–11

Find the Core Word that is spelled correctly and fits best in the blank. Mark your answers in the Answer Rows.

1. You should _____ before the game.
   A resst   B rest   C resd   D rast

2. Wish me _____ before the test.
   F luk   G luc   H luck   J lak

3. The new bridge was very _____.
   A grend   B gran   C grent   D grand

4. What happens if you _____ red and blue paint?
   F blend   G blan   H blant   J blent

5. The _____ of the plane shook.
   A weg   B wing   C weng   D winge

6. Try to _____ the wire around your pencil.
   F bend   G ben   H bint   J bant

7. We must _____ the door before we begin.
   A shat   B shet   C shut   D shudt

8. My mom can _____ us to the movie.
   F driv   G driev   H jriv   J drive

ANSWER ROWS 1. Ⓐ Ⓑ Ⓒ Ⓓ   3. Ⓐ Ⓑ Ⓒ Ⓓ   5. Ⓐ Ⓑ Ⓒ Ⓓ   7. Ⓐ Ⓑ Ⓒ Ⓓ
                2. Ⓕ Ⓖ Ⓗ Ⓙ   4. Ⓕ Ⓖ Ⓗ Ⓙ   6. Ⓕ Ⓖ Ⓗ Ⓙ   8. Ⓕ Ⓖ Ⓗ Ⓙ

Name _____ **Date** _____

Level 2, Lesson 12

Review for Lessons 7–11

Find the underlined part of each sentence that is misspelled. If all the words are correct, choose <u>No mistake</u>. Mark your answers in the Answer Rows.

1. On my <u>trep</u> I <u>met</u> a man wearing a <u>mask</u>.   <u>No mistake</u>.
    A   B   C   D

2. We will <u>rest</u> on the <u>rog</u> before the <u>test</u>.   <u>No mistake</u>.
         F   G   H   J

3. The <u>eg</u> in the <u>nest</u> <u>must</u> be ready to hatch soon.   <u>No mistake</u>.
       A   B   C   D

4. He will <u>drive</u> the <u>truck</u> with the <u>russt</u> on it.   <u>No mistake</u>.
          F   G   H   J

5. She had a <u>plott</u> to <u>dump</u> the <u>plum</u> in the trash.   <u>No mistake</u>.
            A   B   C   D

6. Do you <u>plan</u> to sing a <u>longe</u> <u>song</u>?   <u>No mistake</u>.
          F   G   H   J

7. He was <u>glad</u> he <u>went</u> to soccer <u>camp</u>.   <u>No mistake</u>.
          A   B   C   D

8. <u>Blend</u> two colors to make <u>graiy</u> for the <u>tree</u> trunk. <u>No mistake</u>.
    F   G   H   J

ANSWER ROWS   1. Ⓐ Ⓑ Ⓒ Ⓓ   3. Ⓐ Ⓑ Ⓒ Ⓓ   5. Ⓐ Ⓑ Ⓒ Ⓓ   7. Ⓐ Ⓑ Ⓒ Ⓓ
              2. Ⓕ Ⓖ Ⓗ Ⓙ   4. Ⓕ Ⓖ Ⓗ Ⓙ   6. Ⓕ Ⓖ Ⓗ Ⓙ   8. Ⓕ Ⓖ Ⓗ Ⓙ

Name _____ **Date** _____

Level 2, Lesson 12

Review for Lessons 7-11

Read each phrase. Choose the phrase in which the underlined word is not spelled correctly. Mark your answers in the Answer Rows.

1. A <u>sind</u> a letter
   B <u>bend</u> the stick
   C <u>gray</u> mouse
   D go to <u>camp</u>

2. F sing a <u>song</u>
   G lie down and <u>rest</u>
   H spelling <u>tist</u>
   J <u>must</u> see

3. A a silly <u>grinn</u>
   B study <u>plan</u>
   C <u>drip</u> in the sink
   D clean your <u>desk</u>

4. F bird's <u>nest</u>
   G got <u>stuc</u>
   H good <u>luck</u>
   J <u>blend</u> together

5. A <u>went</u> home
   B not <u>yet</u>
   C <u>long</u> walk
   D drive a <u>truk</u>

6. F after we <u>met</u>
   G <u>junp</u> over
   H <u>rub</u> your head
   J maple <u>tree</u>

7. A <u>blink</u> your eyes
   B painful <u>sting</u>
   C loud <u>blasd</u>
   D <u>fed</u> the cat

8. F <u>mud</u> puddle
   G <u>tog</u> on the rope
   H <u>drum</u> beat
   J <u>glass</u> of water

ANSWER ROWS
1. Ⓐ Ⓑ Ⓒ Ⓓ   3. Ⓐ Ⓑ Ⓒ Ⓓ   5. Ⓐ Ⓑ Ⓒ Ⓓ   7. Ⓐ Ⓑ Ⓒ Ⓓ
2. Ⓕ Ⓖ Ⓗ Ⓙ   4. Ⓕ Ⓖ Ⓗ Ⓙ   6. Ⓕ Ⓖ Ⓗ Ⓙ   8. Ⓕ Ⓖ Ⓗ Ⓙ

Name _____ Date _____

Level 2, Lesson 12
Review for Lessons 7–11

Read each phrase. Choose the phrase in which the underlined word is not spelled correctly for the way it is used in the phrase. Mark your answers in the Answer Rows.

1. A summer <u>camp</u>
   B <u>shut</u> the door
   C <u>went</u> help
   D <u>drive</u> away

2. F write on the <u>blink</u>
   G covered with <u>rust</u>
   H eat a <u>plum</u>
   J <u>drove</u> the car

3. A story <u>plot</u>
   B <u>tree</u> or four
   C wear a <u>mask</u>
   D one <u>plus</u> one

4. F <u>trip</u> and fall
   G shake the <u>rug</u>
   H wood <u>block</u>
   J will <u>met</u> a friend

5. A hasn't been <u>fed</u>
   B robin's <u>egg</u>
   C <u>song</u> a note
   D <u>bend</u> over

6. F covered with <u>mud</u>
   G garbage <u>dump</u>
   H broken <u>glass</u>
   J <u>us</u> your pencil

7. A water the <u>plan</u>
   B flap its <u>wing</u>
   C build a <u>nest</u>
   D be <u>glad</u>

8. F a <u>long</u> slide
   G <u>drip</u> the ball
   H <u>jump</u> rope
   J <u>blast</u> off

ANSWER ROWS
1. Ⓐ Ⓑ Ⓒ Ⓓ   3. Ⓐ Ⓑ Ⓒ Ⓓ   5. Ⓐ Ⓑ Ⓒ Ⓓ   7. Ⓐ Ⓑ Ⓒ Ⓓ
2. Ⓕ Ⓖ Ⓗ Ⓙ   4. Ⓕ Ⓖ Ⓗ Ⓙ   6. Ⓕ Ⓖ Ⓗ Ⓙ   8. Ⓕ Ⓖ Ⓗ Ⓙ

Name _____ Date _____

Level 2, Lesson 12

Review for Lessons 7–11

Use the following Core Words from Lessons 7–11 to complete the puzzle.

Lesson 7
rest
met
bend

Lesson 8
us
mud
rust
must

Lesson 9
grin
drive
grand

Lesson 10
plus
glass
blast

Lesson 11
sting
mask

ACROSS

3. Wet dirt
4. Smile
5. You and me
7. A bee does this
9. Rhymes with *pet*
10. _____ off
11. It holds a drink.
12. Take a nap
13. We came to a _____ in the road.

DOWN

1. _____ a car
2. Rhymes with *dust*
3. Have to
6. Two _____ two is four.
8. We had a _____ time.
9. Worn on Halloween

Name _____ **Date** _____

Level 2, Lesson 13

The /ā/ Sound

Fold the paper in half. Use the blanks to write each word as it is read to you. Then, unfold the paper and correct any mistakes. Practice these words.

1. _____ 1. _ *came*

2. _____ 2. _ *bait*

3. _____ 3. _ *rake*

4. _____ 4. _ *hay*

5. _____ 5. _ *plate*

6. _____ 6. _ *pail*

7. _____ 7. _ *cane*

8. _____ 8. _ *raise*

9. _____ 9. _ *grape*

10. _____ 10. _ *say*

Name _____ **Date** _____

Level 2, Lesson 13

The /ā/ Sound

Follow along as your teacher reads each sentence. Write the Core Words in the correct blanks. Check your spelling.

1. A new teacher _____ and gave us each

   a candy _____.

2. We keep our _____ in a _____.

3. I helped Grandpa _____ the

   _____ in the barn.

4. There is only one _____ left on the

   _____.

5. I _____ my hand

   when I want to _____ something.

Name _____ Date _____

Level 2, Lesson 13

The /ā/ Sound

To find ABC order, look at the first letter of words. If the words start with the same letter, look at the second letters, the third letters, and so on. Write each set of words in ABC order.

CORE WORDS

came
bait
rake
hay
plate
pail
cane
raise
grape
say

came bait cane

1. _____

2. _____

3. _____

hay grape

4. _____

5. _____

plate pail

6. _____

7. _____

raise say rake

8. _____

9. _____

10. _____

Name _____ **Date** _____

Level 2, Lesson 13

The /ā/ Sound

RHYMING WORDS

Unscramble the underlined words in these silly rhyming sentences.

1. Cory <u>caem</u> _____ with the

   same <u>cena</u> _____ as Blaine.

2. Please <u>rsaie</u> _____ the <u>krae</u> _____

   _____, for goodness sake.

3. Put the <u>argpe</u> _____ on

   the <u>tlape</u> _____ or we are

   going to be late.

4. What can a horse <u>ays</u> _____

   while chewing on <u>hya</u> _____?

CORE WORDS

came
bait
rake
hay
plate
pail
cane
raise
grape
say

Name _____ **Date** _____

Level 2, Lesson 13

The /ā/ Sound

SUPER SPELLER WORDS

rainbow   apron   acre

PHONETIC PATTERNS

Write the two different /ā/ spelling patterns in the
Super Speller Words. Then write the Super Speller Word
that has that pattern.

1. _____ _____
   _____

2. _____ _____

LETTER SCRAMBLE

Combine the letters from each box to write a
Super Speller Word.

For example: | ae | ppl | = _apple_

3. | ae | cr | _____

4. | aio | rnbw | _____

5. | ao | prn | _____

Name _____ Date _____

Level 2, Lesson 13

The /ā/ Sound

CROSS-CURRICULAR WORDS

slavery   Spain   state

WORD SORT

Write the Cross-Curricular Word that matches each spelling of the /ā/ sound.

	a		ai
1. _____		3. _____	
2. _____			

WORD PARTS

Write the Cross-Curricular Word that has the smaller word in it.

4. pain _____   5. slave _____

DEFINITIONS

Write the Cross-Curricular Word that fits both meanings.

6. _____ : a land that is part of a country
                    : to tell

Name _____ **Date** _____

Level 2, Lesson 13
The /ā/ Sound

Read the story. Find 8 misspellings and 4 other mistakes in the story. Use all 3 proofreading marks to correct the story. Write the misspelled words correctly on the lines.

Proofreading Marks					
⬭	misspelling	⹀	make a capital letter	⊙	add a period

CORE WORDS

came
bait
rake
hay
plate
pail
cane
raise
grape
say

If the children cam to play, i would sae, "Take that rakke and play a game with me" Then I would take a palle and tell them to follow me. They would rake the haye and pick the grapes. they would dig worms for baite and do all my work. I would lean on my kane. I would not raise my hand to help. I would not even pick one grap

1. _____

2. _____

3. _____

4. _____

5. _____

6. _____

7. _____

8. _____

Name _____   Date _____

Level 2, Lesson 13

The /ā/ Sound

CORE WORDS

came	rake	plate	cane	grape
bait	hay	pail	raise	say

> **Every sentence has two main parts:**
>
> 1. The *subject* is all the words related to the subject. The subject is what or who the sentence is about.
>
> 2. The *verb* is all the words related to the verb. The verb tells what the subject is doing or feeling.

Draw a slash (/) between the subject part and the verb part of the sentence. Then circle the Core Words.

1. The bait in the pail smells terrible.

2. The plate holds a red plum and a green grape.

3. The old rake came from the red barn.

4. The mother and baby elephants raise the food with their trunks.

Name _____   **Date** _____

Level 2, Lesson 14

The /ē/ Sound

Fold the paper in half. Use the blanks to write each word as it is read to you. Then, unfold the paper and correct any mistakes. Practice these words.

1. _____	1.	*deep*
2. _____	2.	*meal*
3. _____	3.	*sheep*
4. _____	4.	*each*
5. _____	5.	*wheel*
6. _____	6.	*treat*
7. _____	7.	*bean*
8. _____	8.	*seen*
9. _____	9.	*team*
10. _____	10.	*dream*

Name _____ **Date** _____

Level 2, Lesson 14
The /ē/ Sound
Follow along as your teacher reads each sentence. Write the Core Words in the correct blanks. Check your spelling.

1. The little _____ fell into a _____ hole.

2. Do you brush your teeth after _____ _____?

3. I had a _____ I climbed Jack's _____ stalk.

4. Have you _____ the _____ from my toy car?

5. We had a special _____ because our school's _____ won the game!

Name _____ Date _____

Level 2, Lesson 14

The /ē/ Sound

The pronunciation key in your Speller Dictionary shows you letters and symbols. The word that appears next to each letter or symbol has the same sound as the letter or symbol.
For example: /ē/ me

CORE WORDS

deep
meal
sheep
each
wheel
treat
bean
seen
team
dream

Use the pronunciation key in your Speller Dictionary to say each word below. Then write the Core Word you said.

1. /tēm/ _____

2. /mēl/ _____

3. /wēl/ _____

4. /bēn/ _____

5. /dēp/ _____

6. /drēm/ _____

7. /shēp/ _____

8. /sēn/ _____

Name _____ Date _____

Level 2, Lesson 14

The /ē/ Sound

PUZZLE

Find the Core Words in this word search.
Use the Core Word list to help you.

CORE WORDS

deep	sheep	wheel	bean	team
meal	each	treat	seen	dream

B	S	V	W	B	D	C	X	S	W
J	E	L	H	E	E	A	C	H	X
H	E	T	E	A	M	P	X	E	Z
N	N	E	E	N	N	M	O	E	K
O	R	I	L	F	D	E	E	P	R
C	T	R	E	A	T	A	V	R	R
D	R	E	A	M	V	L	I	P	K

Name _____ **Date** _____

Level 2, Lesson 14

The /ē/ Sound

SUPER SPELLER WORDS

reason   sweet   steed

WORD SORT

Write the Super Speller Word that matches each spelling of the /ē/ sound.

      ee   **ea**

1. _____   3. _____

2. _____

RHYMING WORDS

Write the Super Speller Word that rhymes with the underlined word in each sentence.

4. I will go and <u>feed</u> my _____.

5. I want a <u>treat</u> that is very _____.

6. The _____ winter is my favorite <u>season</u> is because I like the snow.

Name _____ **Date** _____

Level 2, Lesson 14

The /ē/ Sound

CROSS-CURRICULAR WORDS

area   needs   key

WORD SORT

Write the Cross-Curricular Word that matches each spelling of the /ē/ sound below.

e	ey	ee
1. _____	2. _____	3. _____

LETTER CLUES

Write the missing letters to complete each Cross-Curricular Word.

4. ar____a   6. k____y

5. n_____ds

CONTEXT CLUES

Write the Cross-Curricular Word that fits each situation.

7. There is a large space. _____

8. A door is locked. _____

Name _____ **Date** _____

Level 2, Lesson 14

The /ē/ Sound

Read the story. Find 8 misspellings and 4 other mistakes in the story. Use all 3 proofreading marks to correct the story. Write the misspelled words correctly on the lines.

Proofreading Marks					
⬭	misspelling	＝	make a capital letter	⊙	add a period

CORE WORDS

deep
meal
sheep
each
wheel
treat
bean
seen
team
dream

Ech night I dream about a seep who will not eat. the sheep's mother calls in a tem of cooks The cooks bake a special bean pie. do you think the sheep eats this nice mell? The sheep does not like this bean treet The cooks weel away the pie and bury it six feet dep. This is the saddest sheep I have ever siin!

1. _____   5. _____

2. _____   6. _____

3. _____   7. _____

4. _____   8. _____

Name _____ **Date** _____

Level 2, Lesson 14

The /ē/ Sound

CORE WORDS

deep	sheep	wheel	bean	team
meal	each	treat	seen	dream

Here is a fact about possessive nouns:

Nouns name a person, place, feeling, or thing.
When you want to show that a noun possesses
something, you use an apostrophe (').
For example: *a bee's wing*

Rewrite each description using the noun and an
apostrophe.

1. the beginning of the dream

   _____

   _____

2. the seed of the bean

   _____

   _____

3. the center of the wheel

   _____

   _____

Name _____ **Date** _____

Level 2, Lesson 15

The /ī/ Sound

Fold the paper in half. Use the blanks to write each word as it is read to you. Then, unfold the paper and correct any mistakes. Practice these words.

1. _____	1. *shy*
2. _____	2. *right*
3. _____	3. *wide*
4. _____	4. *light*
5. _____	5. *pine*
6. _____	6. *fight*
7. _____	7. *fly*
8. _____	8. *night*
9. _____	9. *dry*
10. _____	10. *sight*

Name _____ **Date** _____

Level 2, Lesson 15

The /i/ Sound

Follow along as your teacher reads each sentence. Write the Core Words in the correct blanks. Check your spelling.

1. A _____ little mouse hid under the tall

   _____ tree.

2. It's not _____ to shout and

   _____!

3. There was a _____ shining through the

   _____ window.

4. That bird can't _____ until its feathers are

   _____.

5. It is a lovely _____

   to see the stars at _____.

Name _____ **Date** _____

Level 2, Lesson 15
The /i/ Sound
A dictionary lists all the meanings for a word.
Write the Core Word that fits both meanings.

**CORE
WORDS**

shy
right
wide
light
pine
fight
fly
night
dry
sight

1. a. not comfortable around
       other people
    b. easily frightened

    _____

    Core Word: _____

2. a. a lamp
    b. not dark

    _____

    Core Word: _____

3. a. good or correct
    b. opposite of left

    _____

    Core Word: _____

4. a. kind of tree
    b. wish or long for something

    _____

    Core Word: _____

5. a. to move through air with wings
    b. to travel in an aircraft

    _____

    Core Word: _____

Name _____ **Date** _____

Level 2, Lesson 15

The /ī/ Sound

CONTEXT CLUES

Use the Core Words to finish the signs.

All 1. _____

trucks keep to

_____

the 2. _____

To help your

_____

3. _____,

turn on the

_____

4. _____

Do
not

_____

7. _____

your kite at

_____

8. _____

The children are

_____

9. _____

and never

_____

10. _____

Do not put 5. _____ trees

_____

in a 6. _____ forest

**CORE
WORDS**

shy
right
wide
light
pine
fight
fly
night
dry
sight

Name _____ **Date** _____

Level 2, Lesson 15

The /i/ Sound

SUPER SPELLER WORDS

sigh   title   pilot

LETTER CLUES

Write the missing letters to complete each Super Speller Word.

_____ _____

1. t_____tl_____

_____ _____ _____

2. s_____ _____ _____

_____ _____ _____

3. p_____ _____ _____t

CONTEXT CLUES

Write the Super Speller Word to complete each sentence.

_____

4. The _____ of my favorite story is "Little Red Riding Hood."

_____

5. The _____ flies the airplane.

_____

6. A _____ is a noise people make when they are sad.

Name _____ Date _____

Level 2, Lesson 15
The /ī/ Sound
CROSS-CURRICULAR WORDS
vibrate   flight   sky

PHONETIC PATTERNS

Write the Cross-Curricular Word that has the same spelling of the /ī/ sound as each word below.

1. night _____   5. bright _____

2. my _____   6. bite _____

3. pine _____   7. why _____

4. fly _____   8. sight _____

SYNONYMS

Write the Cross-Curricular Word that means nearly the same as each word or phrase below.

9. air _____

10. shake _____

11. airplane trip _____

Name _____ **Date** _____

Level 2, Lesson 15

The /ī/ Sound

Read the story. Find 8 misspellings and 4 other mistakes in the story. Use all 3 proofreading marks to correct the story. Write the misspelled words correctly on the lines.

Proofreading Marks					
⬭	misspelling	≡	make a capital letter	⊙	add a period

CORE WORDS

shy
right
wide
light
pine
fight
fly
night
dry
sight

We will fli in a plane. We will fly right over the city, out to the farms. We will see the wid fields below us. we will fly over a pinn forest.

in the afternoon lite we will see a river and the dri stones beside it. We might even see wild animals in a fite. At nite we will fly back to the city

The view is quite a site If you enjoy the ride, don't be shy!

1. _____   5. _____

2. _____   6. _____

3. _____   7. _____

4. _____   8. _____

Name _____ **Date** _____

Level 2, Lesson 15
The /ī/ Sound

CORE WORDS

shy	wide	pine	fly	dry
right	light	fight	night	sight

Here is some information about pronouns:

Pronouns take the place of nouns. Pronouns show possession. Some possessive pronouns you might use are *my, mine, your, yours, his, her, hers, its, our, ours, their,* and *theirs.*

Use a possessive pronoun to describe these ideas a different way. The first one is done for you.

1. the dog he owns _____ *his dog* _____

2. the sight you have _____

3. the night we enjoy _____

Use a possessive pronoun to write each idea another way.

4. This is her cat. _____

5. This is my shy pet. _____

Name _____ **Date** _____

Level 2, Lesson 16

The /ō/ Sound

Fold the paper in half. Use the blanks to write each word as it is read to you. Then, unfold the paper and correct any mistakes. Practice these words.

#		#	
1.	_____	1.	*poke*
2.	_____	2.	*boat*
3.	_____	3.	*row*
4.	_____	4.	*goat*
5.	_____	5.	*snow*
6.	_____	6.	*toad*
7.	_____	7.	*soap*
8.	_____	8.	*blow*
9.	_____	9.	*coat*
10.	_____	10.	*tow*

Name _____ Date _____

Level 2, Lesson 16

The /ō/ Sound

Follow along as your teacher reads each sentence. Write the Core Words in the correct blanks. Check your spelling.

1. We _____ our _____ on the

   back of our car.

2. I wear a _____ and mittens when I play

   in the _____ .

3. Never _____ a _____ in the

   eye.

4. Please _____ out the candles on your

   cake in a _____ .

5. The _____ jumped in my shower and

   slipped on the _____ .

Name _____ **Date** _____

Level 2, Lesson 16

The /ō/ Sound

Entry words appear in ABC order in the dictionary.

CORE WORDS

poke
boat
row
goat
snow
toad
soap
blow
coat
tow

Write the Core Words in ABC order.

1. _____

2. _____

3. _____

4. _____

5. _____

6. _____

7. _____

8. _____

9. _____

10. _____

Name _____ **Date** _____

Level 2, Lesson 16
The /ō/ Sound
PUZZLE

Find the Core Words in this word search.
Use the Core Word list to help you.

CORE WORDS

poke
boat
row
goat
snow
toad
soap
blow
coat
tow

```
X  G  S  N  O  W
Z  P  O  K  E  T
B  O  A  T  G  O
L  X  P  O  O  A
O  R  O  W  A  D
W  C  O  A  T  X
```

Name _____ Date _____

Level 2, Lesson 16

The /ō/ Sound

SUPER SPELLER WORDS

bowl

oath

doze

WORD SORT

Write the Super Speller Word that matches each spelling pattern of the /ō/ sound.

ow	o_e	oa
1. _____	2. _____	3. _____

SYNONYMS

Write the Super Speller Word that means the same as each word below. Check your answers in a dictionary.

4. promise _____

5. nap _____

ANAGRAMS

Use all the letters in the word below to write a Super Speller Word.

6. blow _____

Name _____ Date _____

Level 2, Lesson 16
The /ō/ Sound
CROSS-CURRICULAR WORDS
echo   glow   coal

WORD BUILDING

Write the Cross-Curricular Word that solves each word problem.

1. charcoal - char = _____

2. glowing - ing = _____

3. echoes - es = _____

RIDDLES

Write the Cross-Curricular Word that answers each riddle.

4. I sound like you, but I am not you. I am your

   _____.

5. I am black, but when you heat me I turn red. I am

   _____.

6. I shine in the dark. I am a beautiful _____.

Name _____ **Date** _____

Level 2, Lesson 16
The /ō/ Sound

Read the story. Find 8 misspellings and 4 other mistakes in the story. Use all 3 proofreading marks to correct the story. Write the misspelled words correctly on the lines.

Proofreading Marks					
⬯	misspelling	≡	make a capital letter	⊙	add a period

CORE WORDS

poke
boat
row
goat
snow
toad
soap
blow
coat
tow

Did you hear about the tode who needed sope? she got in her bote and it started to sno. she began to roe as fast as she could "Oh no! The wind has started to blow," cried the toad.

"You should wear a koat," said a goet The goat offered to towe the toad's boat.

1. _____

2. _____

3. _____

4. _____

5. _____

6. _____

7. _____

8. _____

Name _____ **Date** _____

Level 2, Lesson 16
The /ō/ Sound
CORE WORDS

poke	row	snow	soap	coat
boat	goat	toad	blow	tow

To make a comparison, you can:

1. add *-er* to an adjective when you compare two things. Add *-est* when you compare three or more things.

2. add the word *more* to an adverb when you compare two ways of doing something. Add the word *most* when you compare three or more ways of doing something.

If the underlined adjective or adverb is correct, put a ✔ in the box. If it is incorrect, put an *x* in the box.

1. This is the <u>larger</u> toad in the whole pond. ☐

2. Blow the snow <u>quickly</u>. ☐

3. The goat will poke along <u>most slowly</u> than a horse. ☐

4. This is the <u>nicer</u> coat in the whole store. ☐

5. Your soap is <u>more bubbly</u> than my soap. ☐

6. Is this boat <u>biggest</u> than yours? ☐

Name _____ **Date** _____

Level 2, Lesson 17

The /o͞o/ Sound

Fold the paper in half. Use the blanks to write each word as it is read to you. Then, unfold the paper and correct any mistakes. Practice these words.

1. _____	1.	*tune*
2. _____	2.	*moon*
3. _____	3.	*pool*
4. _____	4.	*zoo*
5. _____	5.	*rude*
6. _____	6.	*soon*
7. _____	7.	*boot*
8. _____	8.	*food*
9. _____	9.	*tube*
10. _____	10.	*room*

Name _____ **Date** _____

Level 2, Lesson 17

The /ōō/ Sound

Follow along as your teacher reads each
sentence. Write the Core Words in the
correct blanks. Check your spelling.

1. The cowboy sang a _____ about a lost

   cowboy _____ !

2. The bright _____ shines into my

   _____ as I sleep.

3. I float on a rubber _____ in our

   swimming _____ .

4. We will go to the _____ _____ .

5. It's _____ to make noise when

   you eat your _____ .

Name _____ Date _____

Level 2, Lesson 17

The /o͞o/ Sound

Many words have more than one meaning.
A dictionary lists all the meanings for a word.

CORE WORDS

tune
moon
pool
zoo
rude
soon
boot
food
tube
room

Write the letter of the meaning that shows how the underlined word is used.

room: **a.** part of a building with walls of its own

b. space

1. Is there <u>room</u> for me on the bench?

   _____

   _____

2. A kitchen is the <u>room</u> for cooking.

   _____

   _____

tune: **a.** a group of musical notes that forms an easy-to-remember unit

b. a song

3. They hum the <u>tune</u> that hasn't any

   _____
   ----
   words. _____

4. "The Itsy Bitsy Spider" is a <u>tune</u> I

   _____
   ----
   learned in school. _____

Name _____ **Date** _____

Level 2, Lesson 17

The /o͞o/ Sound

CONTEXT CLUES

Write the Core Word that finishes each headline. Begin each word with a capital letter.

1. Town to Get a New Swimming

   _____

   _____

2. Spaceship Lands on the

   _____

   _____

3. Restaurant Donates _____

4. Panda Bear Given to the

   _____

   _____

5. Standing _____ Only at Play

   _____

6. _____ Student Sent to Office

   _____

7. Teacher Caught in _____

   on Playground

CORE WORDS

tune
moon
pool
zoo
rude
soon
boot
food
tube
room

Name _____ **Date** _____

Level 2, Lesson 17

The /ōō/ Sound
SUPER SPELLER WORDS

cruel
gloom
costume

LETTER CLUES

Write the missing letters to spell the Super Speller
Words. Then write the words.

_____ _____   _____

1. gl_____ _____m   _____

_____ _____   _____

2. cost_____m_____   _____

_____

3. cr_____el   _____

ANTONYMS

Write the Super Speller Word that means the opposite
of each word.

_____

4. happiness _____

_____

5. kind _____

Name _____ **Date** _____

Level 2, Lesson 17

The /ōō/ Sound

CROSS-CURRICULAR WORDS

cube   unit   rule

LETTER CLUES

Write the missing letters to complete each
Cross-Curricular Word.

1. c_____be   2. _____nit   3. r_____le

PHONETIC PATTERNS

Write the Cross-Curricular Word that has the same
spelling pattern as each word below.

4. cubic _____   6. ruler _____

5. united _____

PLURALS

Add -s to each Cross-Curricular Word to write words
that name more than one.

7. cube _____   9. unit _____

8. rule _____

Name _____ **Date** _____

Level 2, Lesson 17

The /ōō/ Sound

Read the story. Find 8 misspellings and 4 other mistakes in the story. Use all 3 proofreading marks to correct the story. Write the misspelled words correctly on the lines.

Proofreading Marks					
⬭	misspelling	=	make a capital letter	⊙	add a period

CORE WORDS

tune
moon
pool
zoo
rude
soon
boot
food
tube
room

did you ever go to the zu? The worker gives the animals fude. She gives fish to the seals in the poole. she sends some food down a toob.

The worker has one red and one blue boote. As she works, she hums a toone. One song is about the cow that jumped over the mon I love the zoo and want to go back sune

1. _____

2. _____

3. _____

4. _____

5. _____

6. _____

7. _____

8. _____

Name _____ Date _____

Level 2, Lesson 17

The /o͞o/ Sound

CORE WORDS

| tune | pool | rude | boot | tube |
| moon | zoo | soon | food | room |

Common nouns name any person, place, thing, or idea.

List Core Words that name a person, place, thing, or idea.

1. _____

2. _____

3. _____

4. _____

5. _____

6. _____

7. _____

8. _____

Circle the nouns in each sentence.

9. From my room I could see the shining moon.

10. The seals like to swim in a pool at the zoo.

11. I sang my tune into the tube.

Name _____ **Date** _____

Level 2, Lesson 18

Review for Lessons 13–17

Fold the paper in half. Use the blanks to write each word as it is read to you. Then, unfold the paper and correct any mistakes. Practice these words.

1. _____		1.	*zoo*
2. _____		2.	*blow*
3. _____		3.	*light*
4. _____		4.	*team*
5. _____		5.	*raise*
6. _____		6.	*sheep*
7. _____		7.	*sight*
8. _____		8.	*soap*
9. _____		9.	*moon*
10. _____		10.	*plate*

Name _____ **Date** _____

Level 2, Lesson 18

Review for Lessons 13-17

Follow along as your teacher reads each sentence. Write the Core Words in the correct blanks. Check your spelling.

1. Are there _____ at the _____?

2. Please _____ the _____ a little so

   I can see.

3. I like to _____ _____ bubbles.

4. At the _____ of our _____,

   everyone started to clap.

5. I could see the full _____ in the clean

   _____.

Name _____ Date _____

Level 2, Lesson 18

Review for Lessons 13–17

Read each answer. Fill in the space in the Answer Rows for the choice that has a spelling error. If there is no mistake, fill in the last answer space.

1. A hay
   B toob
   C fight
   D soap
   E (No mistake)

2. F cote
   G grape
   H dream
   J shy
   K (No mistake)

3. A boat
   B pool
   C playt
   D treat
   E (No mistake)

4. F flie
   G blow
   H wheel
   J wide
   K (No mistake)

5. A deap
   B right
   C row
   D zoo
   E (No mistake)

6. F pail
   G bean
   H nyte
   J food
   K (No mistake)

7. A room
   B came
   C meal
   D sae
   E (No mistake)

8. F goat
   G rude
   H cane
   J seen
   K (No mistake)

ANSWER ROWS   1. Ⓐ Ⓑ Ⓒ Ⓓ Ⓔ   3. Ⓐ Ⓑ Ⓒ Ⓓ Ⓔ   5. Ⓐ Ⓑ Ⓒ Ⓓ Ⓔ   7. Ⓐ Ⓑ Ⓒ Ⓓ Ⓔ
              2. Ⓕ Ⓖ Ⓗ Ⓙ Ⓚ   4. Ⓕ Ⓖ Ⓗ Ⓙ Ⓚ   6. Ⓕ Ⓖ Ⓗ Ⓙ Ⓚ   8. Ⓕ Ⓖ Ⓗ Ⓙ Ⓚ

Name _____ **Date** _____

Level 2, Lesson 18

Review for Lessons 13–17

First Day of School

How did you feel when you came to school for the first day of second grade? Write about it. Use as many Core Words as you can.

Follow these steps:

1. Begin by telling what you are writing about.

2. Tell how you felt and what you were thinking.

3. Were you looking forward to seeing your friends? Were you in a hurry to meet your teacher? Were you worried about anything?

4. Tell how you felt by the end of the school day.

Remember...

- Take some time to plan.

- Write down any ideas you have on scrap paper.

- Write your paper.

- Look over your work. Check it for spelling and other mistakes. Fix any that you find.

Name _____ **Date** _____

Level 2, Lesson 18

Review for Lessons 13–17

Find the Core Word that is spelled correctly and fits best in the blank. Mark your answers in the Answer Rows.

1. Do you _____ cows on your farm?
   A rase   B raiz   C rais   D raise

2. The old _____ had a broken spoke.
   F weel   G wheel   H whele   J wheal

3. How _____ is the ribbon?
   A wide   B wid   C wied   D wyd

4. The _____ will sink if there is a hole.
   F bote   G bot   H boat   J boet

5. The _____ was hidden behind a cloud.
   A mune   B mun   C moun   D moon

6. She spilled _____ juice on her pants.
   F grap   G graip   H grape   J graep

7. Did you have a good _____ last night?
   A dream   B dreme   C dreem   D drem

8. The bright _____ is shining in my eyes.
   F lite   G light   H ligt   J liht

ANSWER ROWS   1. Ⓐ Ⓑ Ⓒ Ⓓ   3. Ⓐ Ⓑ Ⓒ Ⓓ   5. Ⓐ Ⓑ Ⓒ Ⓓ   7. Ⓐ Ⓑ Ⓒ Ⓓ
               2. Ⓕ Ⓖ Ⓗ Ⓙ   4. Ⓕ Ⓖ Ⓗ Ⓙ   6. Ⓕ Ⓖ Ⓗ Ⓙ   8. Ⓕ Ⓖ Ⓗ Ⓙ

Name _____ **Date** _____

Level 2, Lesson 18

Review for Lessons 13–17

Find the underlined part of each sentence that is misspelled. If all the words are correct, choose <u>No mistake</u>. Mark your answers in the Answer Rows.

1. If you <u>row</u> the <u>boat</u>, I will <u>bait</u> your hook.　<u>No mistake</u>.
　　　 A　　　　 B　　　　 C　　　　　　　　 D

2. I am too <u>shiy</u> to <u>say</u> the <u>right</u> thing.　<u>No mistake</u>.
　　　　　 F　　　 G　　　 H　　　　　　 J

3. <u>Rake</u> the <u>haiy</u> and give it to the <u>goat</u>.　<u>No mistake</u>.
　 A　　　 B　　　　　　　　　 C　　　　 D

4. The <u>teem</u> will <u>raise</u> money to buy <u>tube</u> socks.　<u>No mistake</u>.
　　　 F　　　 G　　　　　　　　　 H　　　　 J

5. Have you ever <u>seen</u> a <u>toad</u> in your <u>rom</u>?　<u>No mistake</u>.
　　　　　　　 A　　　 B　　　　 C　　　　 D

6. I <u>came</u> to the <u>pule</u> and went in the <u>deep</u> water.　<u>No mistake</u>.
　　 F　　　　　 G　　　　　　　　 H　　　　　 J

7. Do not <u>poak</u> at the <u>sheep</u> with that <u>cane</u>.　<u>No mistake</u>.
　　　 A　　　　 B　　　　　 C　　　　 D

8. We gave a name to <u>each</u> <u>pine</u> tree in <u>siht</u>.　<u>No mistake</u>.
　　　　　　　　 F　　 G　　　　 H　　　 J

ANSWER ROWS　1. Ⓐ Ⓑ Ⓒ Ⓓ　3. Ⓐ Ⓑ Ⓒ Ⓓ　5. Ⓐ Ⓑ Ⓒ Ⓓ　7. Ⓐ Ⓑ Ⓒ Ⓓ
　　　　　　　2. Ⓕ Ⓖ Ⓗ Ⓙ　4. Ⓕ Ⓖ Ⓗ Ⓙ　6. Ⓕ Ⓖ Ⓗ Ⓙ　8. Ⓕ Ⓖ Ⓗ Ⓙ

Name _____ **Date** _____

Level 2, Lesson 18

Review for Lessons 13–17

Read each phrase. Choose the phrase in which the underlined word is not spelled correctly. Mark your answers in the Answer Rows.

1. A <u>shy</u> child
   B <u>toon</u> the piano
   C <u>poke</u> with a stick
   D <u>deep</u> in the woods

2. F <u>caim</u> home
   G <u>right</u> hand
   H <u>bait</u> the hook
   J float the <u>boat</u>

3. A half <u>moon</u>
   B count <u>sheep</u>
   C <u>rayk</u> the leaves
   D <u>wide</u> road

4. F home <u>plate</u>
   G sit in a <u>roe</u>
   H spin the <u>wheel</u>
   J <u>pine</u> tree

5. A <u>snow</u> boots
   B <u>pail</u> of water
   C don't be <u>rude</u>
   D a sweet <u>treet</u>

6. F a hopping <u>toad</u>
   G very <u>soon</u>
   H <u>fite</u> against crime
   J sugar <u>cane</u>

7. A green <u>bean</u>
   B bar of <u>sope</u>
   C <u>fly</u> away
   D lost a <u>boot</u>

8. F <u>raise</u> your hand
   G good <u>night</u>
   H have you <u>seen</u>
   J noon <u>meel</u>

ANSWER ROWS   1. Ⓐ Ⓑ Ⓒ Ⓓ   3. Ⓐ Ⓑ Ⓒ Ⓓ   5. Ⓐ Ⓑ Ⓒ Ⓓ   7. Ⓐ Ⓑ Ⓒ Ⓓ
              2. Ⓕ Ⓖ Ⓗ Ⓙ   4. Ⓕ Ⓖ Ⓗ Ⓙ   6. Ⓕ Ⓖ Ⓗ Ⓙ   8. Ⓕ Ⓖ Ⓗ Ⓙ

Name _____ **Date** _____

Level 2, Lesson 18

Review for Lessons 13-17

Read each phrase. Choose the phrase in which the underlined word is not spelled correctly for the way it is used in the phrase. Mark your answers in the Answer Rows.

1. A broken <u>plate</u>
   B <u>pail</u> yellow
   C swimming <u>pool</u>
   D <u>hay</u> for sale

2. F <u>bean</u> to school
   G turn on the <u>light</u>
   H <u>each</u> person
   J milk the <u>goat</u>

3. A go to the <u>zoo</u>
   B inner <u>tube</u>
   C in the hot <u>soon</u>
   D <u>say</u> your name

4. F a bad <u>dream</u>
   G zip your <u>coat</u>
   H out of <u>sight</u>
   J second <u>seen</u>

5. A buy a <u>rake</u>
   B <u>right</u> your name
   C <u>sheep</u> in the field
   D <u>poke</u> a hole

6. F safety <u>pine</u>
   G full of <u>food</u>
   H out of <u>tune</u>
   J <u>blow</u> in the wind

7. A stay <u>dry</u>
   B on the <u>team</u>
   C <u>night</u> sky
   D read a <u>boot</u>

8. F stub your <u>tow</u>
   G <u>deep</u> blue sea
   H use a <u>cane</u>
   J <u>fly</u> on a jet

ANSWER ROWS   1. Ⓐ Ⓑ Ⓒ Ⓓ   3. Ⓐ Ⓑ Ⓒ Ⓓ   5. Ⓐ Ⓑ Ⓒ Ⓓ   7. Ⓐ Ⓑ Ⓒ Ⓓ
              2. Ⓕ Ⓖ Ⓗ Ⓙ   4. Ⓕ Ⓖ Ⓗ Ⓙ   6. Ⓕ Ⓖ Ⓗ Ⓙ   8. Ⓕ Ⓖ Ⓗ Ⓙ

Lesson 18 Review 145

Name _____ Date _____

Level 2, Lesson 18
Review for Lessons 13–17

Use the following Core Words from Lessons 13–17 to complete the puzzle.

Lesson 13
raise
plate

Lesson 14
team
sheep
dream
wheel
deep

Lesson 15
wide
sight

Lesson 16
soap
snow
row
boat
blow

Lesson 17
moon

ACROSS
1. A dish
3. Floats on water
4. Broad
7. Full-grown lamb
9. To see
10. I come out at night
11. Way down
12. Move a boat across water

DOWN
2. Baseball group
3. _____ a bubble
5. When you sleep
6. Lift up
7. Used with water
8. Spins around
9. Type of flake

Name _____ **Date** _____

Level 2, Lesson 19

Words with *wh* and *sh*

Fold the paper in half. Use the blanks to write each word as it is read to you. Then, unfold the paper and correct any mistakes. Practice these words.

1. _____	1. *what*
2. _____	2. *clash*
3. _____	3. *shock*
4. _____	4. *while*
5. _____	5. *shame*
6. _____	6. *flash*
7. _____	7. *where*
8. _____	8. *shine*
9. _____	9. *why*
10. _____	10. *shore*

Name _____ **Date** _____

Level 2, Lesson 19

Words with *wh* and *sh*

Follow along as your teacher reads each sentence. Write the Core Words in the correct blanks. Check your spelling.

1. Do you know _____ we will do if

   the sun doesn't _____?

2. Could you hear the cymbals _____ from

   _____ you were sitting?

3. Can a _____ of lightning give someone a

   _____?

4. I swam every day _____ we were at the

   _____.

5. _____ does she feel _____?

Name _____ **Date** _____

Level 2, Lesson 19
Words with *wh* and *sh*

An entry word is the word you look up in a dictionary. A definition tells you what the word means. Many entry words have more than one definition.

CORE WORDS

what
clash
shock
while
shame
flash
where
shine
why
shore

Look up the word *shore* in your Speller Dictionary. Answer the following questions.

1. What is the entry word?

   _____

   - - - - - - - - - - - - - - - - -

   _____

2. How many definitions does it have?

   _____

   - - - - - - - - - - - - - - - - -

   _____

3. What is the second definition?

   _____

   - - - - - - - - - - - - - - - - -

   _____

Now look up the entry for *shame.*

4. What is the entry word?

   _____

   - - - - - - - - - - - - - - - - -

   _____

5. How many definitions does it have?

   - - - - - - - - - - - - - - - - -

   _____

Name _____ **Date** _____

Level 2, Lesson 19
Words with *wh* and *sh*
RIDDLES

Write the Core Word that goes with each clue. Then use the letters in the boxes to answer the question at the end.

1. during or in the time that

2. reason or purpose

3. feeling of guilt

4. beach

5. to give light

6. What word begins a question about

   location?

CORE WORDS

what
clash
shock
while
shame
flash
where
shine
why
shore

Name _____ Date _____

Level 2, Lesson 19

Words with *wh* and *sh*

SUPER SPELLER WORDS

smallish

whisk

shale

WORD SORT

Sort the Super Speller Words according to the spelling patterns below.

sh	wh
1. _____	3. _____
2. _____	

DEFINITIONS

Write the Super Speller Word that fits each meaning.

4. a rock with many layers _____

5. to move something quickly _____

6. little _____

Name _____ **Date** _____

Level 2, Lesson 19

Words with *wh* and *sh*

CROSS-CURRICULAR WORDS

showers
shone
wheat

CLASSIFYING

Write the Cross-Curricular Word or words that fit each group.

Begins with sh   **Begins with wh**

_____   _____

1. _____   2. _____

   _____

3. _____

ANTONYMS

Write the Cross-Curricular Word that means nearly the opposite of the underlined words.

4. <u>Sunshine</u> hit me on the head, so I got out my

   _____

   umbrella. _____

5. The sun <u>went dark</u>, so I put on my sunglasses.

   _____

   _____

Name _____ **Date** _____

Level 2, Lesson 19

Words with *wh* and *sh*

Read the story. Find 8 misspellings and 4 other mistakes in the story. Use all 3 proofreading marks to correct the story. Write the misspelled words correctly on the lines.

Proofreading Marks					
⬭	misspelling	⹀	make a capital letter	⊙	add a period

sheri and Shawn stood on the shor and looked at the sky They saw a flasth of light The two girls heard a klash. Sheri felt a shok go through her. "Wat is going on?" she asked.

"I wish the sun would shin," said Shawn. "It went away whil we were swimming"

"Whi don't we go inside before it rains," said Shawn.

CORE WORDS

what
clash
shock
while
shame
flash
where
shine
why
shore

1. _____

2. _____

3. _____

4. _____

5. _____

6. _____

7. _____

8. _____

Name _____ Date _____

Level 2, Lesson 19

Words with *wh* and *sh*
CORE WORDS

what	shock	shame	where	why
clash	while	flash	shine	shore

Here is some information about proper nouns:

1. A proper noun names a special person, a special place, or a special thing.

2. A proper noun begins with a capital letter: *Elaine, France, Sunburst Orange Drink*, and *Bronx Zoo*.

Write a proper noun for every blank. Then circle the Core Words.

My name is _____. In a flash, I can solve

a mystery. My teacher, _____, wants me to

figure out where the class gerbil went. Its name is

_____. First I will shine a flashlight in the halls

of _____ School. While I shine the light, I do

not want to shock our pet. I want to know why it is hiding.

Name _____ **Date** _____

Level 2, Lesson 20

Words with *ch* and *th*

Fold the paper in half. Use the blanks to write each word as it is read to you. Then, unfold the paper and correct any mistakes. Practice these words.

1. _____	1. *bath*
2. _____	2. *peach*
3. _____	3. *tooth*
4. _____	4. *thin*
5. _____	5. *choke*
6. _____	6. *much*
7. _____	7. *with*
8. _____	8. *chick*
9. _____	9. *teach*
10. _____	10. *thank*

Name _____ **Date** _____

Level 2, Lesson 20

Words with *ch* and *th*

Follow along as your teacher reads each sentence. Write the Core Words in the correct blanks. Check your spelling.

_____

1. Yes, _____ you, I would like to take a _____ .

2. Please cut the _____ into _____ slices.

3. How _____ did it hurt when you lost your _____ ?

4. You could _____ _____ all that food in your mouth!

5. The mother hen will _____ her baby _____ how to find food.

Name _____ **Date** _____

Level 2, Lesson 20

Words with *ch* and *th*

A dictionary entry gives an example sentence to help explain what a word means.

much /much/ *adjective* great in amount or degree. *I don't have much money left after buying that gift.*

CORE WORDS

bath
peach
tooth
thin
choke
much
with
chick
teach
thank

Look up these Core Words in your Speller Dictionary. Write a sample sentence of your own for each word.

1. peach _____
_____
_____

2. teach _____
_____
_____

3. chick _____
_____
_____

4. choke _____
_____

Name _____ Date _____

Level 2, Lesson 20

Words with *ch* and *th*

CONTEXT CLUES

Use the Core Word list to complete these tongue twisters.

1. Mary and Martin miss Mugsy the Mutt

   _____

   very _____ .

   CORE WORDS

2. Patti Powel planted a perfect

   _____

   _____ pit under the purple

   primrose patch.

   bath
   peach
   tooth
   thin
   choke
   much
   with
   chick
   teach
   thank

3. The_____ won't _____

   on chopped cherries.

4. Why is Wally watering the weeds

   _____

   _____Wendy?

   _____

5. Tory taught tiny Tina that _____

   decay is terrible trouble.

Name _____ Date _____

Level 2, Lesson 20

Words with *ch* and *th*

SUPER SPELLER WORDS

underneath

pitcher

churn

LETTER CLUES

Write the missing letters to complete the
Super Speller Words.

1. undernea_____ _____   3. pit_____ _____er

2. _____ _____urn

DEFINITIONS

Write the Super Speller Words that fit both meanings.

4. _____ : A baseball player who throws the
ball to the batter.

: A container used for pouring
liquids such as water, milk, or
juice.

5. _____ : A machine used to make butter.

: To move roughly.

Name _____ Date _____

Level 2, Lesson 20

Words with *ch* and *th*

CROSS-CURRICULAR WORDS

chief   Earth   church

ANALOGIES

Write the Cross-Curricular Word that completes each analogy.

1. *group* is to *leader* as *tribe* is to _____

2. *children* is to *homes* as *people* is to

   _____

   _____

3. *schoolbooks* is to *school* as *prayer books* is to

   _____

   _____

DEFINITIONS

Write the Cross-Curricular Word that fits each meaning.

_____

4. a planet _____

_____

5. a place where people pray _____

_____

6. a person who leads _____

Name _____ Date _____

Level 2, Lesson 20

Words with *ch* and *th*

Read the story. Find 8 misspellings and 4 other mistakes in the story. Use all 3 proofreading marks to correct the story. Write the misspelled words correctly on the lines.

Proofreading Marks					
⬭	misspelling	=	make a capital letter	⊙	add a period

Take a bathey every day. Do not drink the bath water, or you might chok. Wash your face whith a cloth. Brush every tuth.

Do not try to tech a chick to ski. do you think a chik could hold ski poles? chicks do not like the snow very mush. they will thunk you if you keep them warm

CORE WORDS

bath
peach
tooth
thin
choke
much
with
chick
teach
thank

1. _____   5. _____

2. _____   6. _____

3. _____   7. _____

4. _____   8. _____

Name _____ **Date** _____

Level 2, Lesson 20

Words with *ch* and *th*

CORE WORDS

bath	tooth	choke	with	teach
peach	thin	much	chick	thank

Here is some information about pronouns:

1. Pronouns take the place of nouns.

2. Some pronouns you might use are *I, me, you, he, him, she, her, it, we, us, they,* and *them.*

Complete the story with pronouns.

Phillip was in the woods. _____ stopped

at a house. A woman opened the door and said,

"Who are _____?" She was thin.

_____ carried a basket. She showed

_____ a chick in her basket. "I have many,"

she said. "_____ are magic. Take

_____."

Name _____ **Date** _____

Level 2, Lesson 21

The /är/ Sound

Fold the paper in half. Use the blanks to write each
word as it is read to you. Then, unfold the paper and
correct any mistakes. Practice these words.

1. _____   1. *art*

2. _____   2. *yard*

3. _____   3. *barn*

4. _____   4. *park*

5. _____   5. *hard*

6. _____   6. *cart*

7. _____   7. *dark*

8. _____   8. *farm*

9. _____   9. *shark*

10. _____   10. *sharp*

Name _____ **Date** _____

Level 2, Lesson 21

The /är/ Sound

Follow along as your teacher reads each sentence. Write the Core Words in the correct blanks. Check your spelling.

1. Is it _____ to make clay people in

    _____ class?

2. Today I'll play outside in my _____ or in

    the _____.

3. Come see the horses in the _____ on

    Grandpa's _____.

4. A _____ has very _____ teeth!

5. A little pony pulled the _____ down a

    _____ road.

Name _____ **Date** _____

Level 2, Lesson 21

The /är/ Sound

The meanings of some words are easier to understand by seeing pictures. That's why some dictionaries give pictures for some words. The picture is called an illustration. Beside every illustration is the name of the entry word and the number of the definition.

CORE WORDS

art
yard
barn
park
hard
cart
dark
farm
shark
sharp

Look at the entry for *cart*. Draw an illustration in the box to show the first, or noun, meaning of the word.

cart /kärt/ *noun* a strong wagon with two wheels that is used to carry a load. Carts are usually pulled by horses, mules, or oxen. —*verb* to carry or transport.

Name _____ Date _____

Level 2, Lesson 21

The /är/ Sound

PUZZLE

Find the Core Words in this word search.
Use the Core Word list to help you.

CORE WORDS

art	barn	hard	dark	shark
yard	park	cart	farm	sharp

H	M	B	E	O	Y	A	R	D	U
B	L	S	M	B	A	R	N	O	N
M	U	L	A	Y	H	T	R	C	E
T	S	E	S	H	T	P	P	A	O
S	H	A	R	K	A	H	A	R	D
D	A	M	Y	R	F	X	R	T	Q
M	R	K	F	D	A	R	K	S	R
E	P	O	R	I	R	H	T	T	A
H	C	S	H	T	M	L	O	W	D

Name _____ Date _____

Level 2, Lesson 21

The /är/ Sound

SUPER SPELLER WORDS

harmless

parlor

charming

PHONETIC PATTERNS

Write the Super Speller Words in ABC order and circle the letters that spell the /är/ sound in each.

1. _____   3. _____

2. _____

BASE WORDS

Write the base word of these Super Speller Words.

4. harmless _____

5. charming _____

Which of the Super Speller Words means the opposite of its base word?

6. _____

Name _____ Date _____

Level 2, Lesson 21

The /är/ Sound

CROSS-CURRICULAR WORDS

part   lark   carp

PHONETIC PATTERNS

Write the Cross-Curricular Words and circle the spelling pattern that is the same in each.

1. _____   3. _____

2. _____

CLASSIFYING

Write the Cross-Curricular Word that belongs with each group.

4. fish, lake, river, _____

5. bird, sky, fly, _____

6. piece, bit, half, _____

LETTER SCRAMBLE

Cross out the letters that don't belong to find the hidden Cross-Curricular Words.

7. carpenter _____   8. partner _____

Name _____ **Date** _____

Level 2, Lesson 21

The /är/ Sound

Read the story. Find 8 misspellings and 4 other mistakes in the story. Use all 3 proofreading marks to correct the story. Write the misspelled words correctly on the lines.

Proofreading Marks					
⬭	misspelling	=	make a capital letter	⊙	add a period

one night we went to a faarm. It was darck.

We had to parck our car in the road.

It is hard to see in the dark Doing it is an artt.

You need sharpe eyes

After a little while, I could see the brn. There

were two horses in the yerd near it. In the

morning, they would pull the farmer's cartte

CORE WORDS

art
yard
barn
park
hard
cart
dark
farm
shark
sharp

1. _____

2. _____

3. _____

4. _____

5. _____

6. _____

7. _____

8. _____

Name _____   **Date** _____

Level 2, Lesson 21

The /är/ Sound

CORE WORDS

art	barn	hard	dark	shark
yard	park	cart	farm	sharp

Here is some information about verbs:

A verb is a part of speech that shows action. Here are some action verbs: *pull, run, whisper, jump, spell, write,* and *listen.*

Underline four action verbs in the poem.

One day when I played in the park,
The sky changed from light to dark.
I bumped into something I thought was a cart.
But it was really a strange work of art!

Answer the questions. Circle the verb in your answer.

1. What happens when you feel something sharp?

_____

- -

2. What is something that happens on a farm?

_____

- -

Name _____ **Date** _____

Level 2, Lesson 22

The /ûr/ and /or/ Sounds

Fold the paper in half. Use the blanks to write each word as it is read to you. Then, unfold the paper and correct any mistakes. Practice these words.

1. _____	1. *bird*
2. _____	2. *more*
3. _____	3. *shirt*
4. _____	4. *horse*
5. _____	5. *first*
6. _____	6. *for*
7. _____	7. *girl*
8. _____	8. *horn*
9. _____	9. *dirt*
10. _____	10. *short*

Name _____ **Date** _____

Level 2, Lesson 22

The /ûr/ and /or/ Sounds

Follow along as your teacher reads each sentence. Write the Core Words in the correct blanks. Check your spelling.

1. A nest is a home _____ a

   _____

   _____ .

2. This _____ eats _____ hay

   than the other ones.

3. I got mud and _____ on my new blue

   _____ !

4. Marcy was the _____ _____

   in line today.

5. The _____ player blew a

   _____ "toot-toot."

Name _____ Date _____

Level 2, Lesson 22

The /ûr/ and /or/ Sounds

Dictionary entries may have an example sentence to explain the meaning of a word. Look up four Core Words. Write an example sentence of your own.

CORE WORDS

bird
more
shirt
horse
first
for
girl
horn
dirt
short

1. _____
_____
_____
_____

2. _____
_____
_____
_____

3. _____
_____
_____
_____

4. _____
_____
_____
_____

Name _____ **Date** _____

Level 2, Lesson 22

The /ûr/ and /or/ Sounds

PUZZLE

Use the Core Words to do the crossword puzzle.

Across

5. The cart was pulled by a _____.

7. Not a boy

8. I made this _____ you.

9. Today I will wear my blue _____.

10. We like to dig in _____.

Down

1. "May I have some _____, please?"

2. Blow your _____.

3. Not tall

4. I finished _____ in the race!

6. A robin is a _____.

CORE WORDS

bird
more
shirt
horse
first
for
girl
horn
dirt
short

Name _____ **Date** _____

Level 2, Lesson 22

The /ûr/ and /or/ Sounds

SUPER SPELLER WORDS

explore   firm   dormitory

WORD SORT

Write the Super Speller Word that has each spelling pattern.

or	**ir**
1. _____	3. _____
2. _____	

CONTEXT CLUES

Write the Super Speller Word to complete each sentence.

4. Ben likes to _____ new places and see

   what he can find.

5. Some people sleep in a _____ .

6. The opposite of *soft* is _____ .

Name _____ Date _____

Level 2, Lesson 22

The /ûr/ and /or/ Sounds

CROSS-CURRICULAR WORDS

spores   tornado   birch

PHONETIC PATTERNS

Write the Cross-Curricular Word that has the same spelling pattern as each pair of words below.

1. bird, birth, _____

2. sport, sportsman, _____

3. torn, torch, _____

CONTEXT CLUES

Write the Cross-Curricular Word that best completes each sentence.

4. My sister and I planted a _____ tree in our backyard.

5. In spring, you can see tiny _____ floating in the air.

6. A wild _____ blew apart our barn.

Name _____ **Date** _____

Level 2, Lesson 22

The /ûr/ and /or/ Sounds

Read the story. Find 8 misspellings and 3 other mistakes in the story. Use all 3 proofreading marks to correct the story. Write the misspelled words correctly on the lines.

Proofreading Marks					
⬭	misspelling	≡	make a capital letter	⊙	add a period

"Let's be the frist ones to look around the farm," my sister called.

I buttoned up my shert and ran outside "Look at that pretty brid," I said. "It's digging in the durt I guess it's looking fore worms. Watch out, worms!"

"Are there any mor animals?" my sister asked.

"There is a brown hors," I told her. "look at the sheep with just one hone!"

CORE WORDS

bird
more
shirt
horse
first
for
girl
horn
dirt
short

1. _____

2. _____

3. _____

4. _____

5. _____

6. _____

7. _____

8. _____

Name _____ Date _____

Level 2, Lesson 22
The /ûr/ and /or/ Sounds
CORE WORDS

bird	shirt	first	girl	dirt
more	horse	for	horn	short

Here is some information about adjectives:

1. Adjectives describe nouns and pronouns.

2. An adjective is a part of speech that helps paint a picture in your mind.

Read this page from a school newspaper. Circle the nine adjectives.

After lunch our favorite reporter went to the playground. It was a beautiful day. Happy children played everywhere. Suddenly, a bird began to chirp. The reporter did not listen to the first sounds. Our smart reporter began to look around when he heard more chirps.

A strange creature was found in the dirt behind the building. It was a very short horse. A kind teacher told her it was a pony. The children enjoyed rides all afternoon.

Name _____ **Date** _____

Level 2, Lesson 23
Easily Misspelled Words

Fold the paper in half. Use the blanks to write each word as it is read to you. Then, unfold the paper and correct any mistakes. Practice these words.

1. _____   1. *does*

2. _____   2. *were*

3. _____   3. *every*

4. _____   4. *very*

5. _____   5. *give*

6. _____   6. *live*

7. _____   7. *thing*

8. _____   8. *your*

9. _____   9. *many*

10. _____   10. *who*

Name _____ Date _____

Level 2, Lesson 23

Easily Misspelled Words

Follow along as your teacher reads each sentence. Write the Core Words in the correct blanks. Check your spelling.

_____   _____

1. Tell me, _____ that boy _____

   next door to you?

   _____   _____

2. There _____ _____ people at

   the party.

   _____   _____

3. I _____ my dad a big hug _____

   night.

   _____   _____

4. This strange _____ is not _____

   pretty!

   _____   _____

5. Do you know _____ made _____

   lunch today?

Name _____ **Date** _____

Level 2, Lesson 23

Easily Misspelled Words

There are two words at the top of each dictionary page called guide words. Guide words tell you the first and last word on that page.

CORE WORDS

does
were
every
very
give
live
thing
your
many
who

Look at the guide words below. Write the Core Word or Words that belong on that dictionary page.

stripe/tip
_____
1. - - - - - - - - - - -
_____

frog/glue
_____
4. - - - - - - - - - - -
_____

van/when
_____
2. - - - - - - - - - - -
_____

dive/family
_____
5. - - - - - - - - - - -
_____

wind/zebra
_____
3. - - - - - - - - - - -
_____

Name _____ **Date** _____

Level 2, Lesson 23

Easily Misspelled Words

LETTER SCRAMBLE

How many Core Words can you make from these letters? Use the Core Word list to help you.

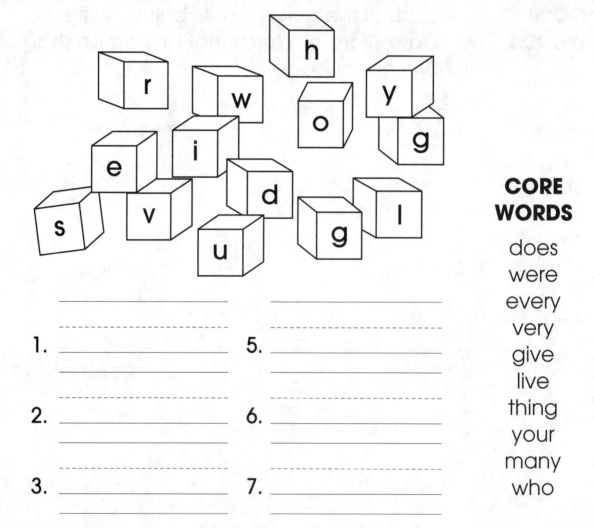

CORE WORDS

does
were
every
very
give
live
thing
your
many
who

1. _____   5. _____

2. _____   6. _____

3. _____   7. _____

4. _____   8. _____

Name _____ **Date** _____

Level 2, Lesson 23

Easily Misspelled Words

SUPER SPELLER WORDS

elastic   lettuce   skillet

SYLLABLES

Write the missing syllables in the Super Speller Words.
Then write the words.

1. skil_____   _____

2. _____las_____   _____

3. let_____   _____

RIDDLES

Write the Super Speller Words that go with these clues.

Which two Super Speller Words have double
consonants?

4. _____   5. _____

Which Super Speller Word has the following smaller
word in it?

6. last _____

Name _____ Date _____

Level 2, Lesson 23
Easily Misspelled Words
CROSS-CURRICULAR WORDS
idea   fuel   teepee

PHONETIC PATTERNS

Write the Cross-Curricular Word that starts with a vowel.

1. _____

Write the Cross-Curricular Word that is one syllable and has two vowels together.

2. _____

Write the Cross-Curricular Word that has four of the same vowel.

3. _____

LETTER SCRAMBLE

Cross out the letters to find the hidden Cross-Curricular Words. Write each word on the lines.

4. ghafuelite _____

5. steephteepeeaie _____

Name _____ Date _____

Level 2, Lesson 23

Easily Misspelled Words

Read the story. Find 8 misspellings and 4 other mistakes in the story. Use all 3 proofreading marks to correct the story. Write the misspelled words correctly on the lines.

Proofreading Marks					
⬭	misspelling	＝	make a capital letter	⊙	add a period

Dear Jenna,

   I was vary happy to get your letter ! wish we did not liv so far away. Dose your brother remember me? My mom said we wer going on a trip next week. She did not say whoo we were going to visit. Evry afternoon I go to the park The best ting is the swings. there are meny children there.

   Your friend,

   jake

CORE WORDS

does
were
every
very
give
live
thing
your
many
who

1. _____

2. _____

3. _____

4. _____

5. _____

6. _____

7. _____

8. _____

Name _____ Date _____

Level 2, Lesson 23

Easily Misspelled Words

CORE WORDS

does	every	give	thing	many
were	very	live	your	who

Here is some information about adverbs:

An adverb is a part of speech that describes verbs. To find an adverb, look at the verb, then ask *how* or *where*.

Alex ran quickly.

The word *quickly* tells how Alex ran.

Underline the adverb in each sentence. Then circle the Core Words.

1. Does your friend talk loudly?

2. We were in the park when many clouds suddenly raced by us.

3. Every fish swam quietly through the water.

4. This thing is an old toy I store safely on my shelf.

5. Who is the person who ran quickly in the hall?

Name _____ **Date** _____

Level 2, Lesson 24

Review for Lessons 19–23

Fold the paper in half. Use the blanks to write each word as it is read to you. Then, unfold the paper and correct any mistakes. Practice these words.

1. _____	1.	*where*
2. _____	2.	*peach*
3. _____	3.	*sharp*
4. _____	4.	*horse*
5. _____	5.	*thin*
6. _____	6.	*clash*
7. _____	7.	*with*
8. _____	8.	*cart*
9. _____	9.	*dirt*
10. _____	10.	*every*

Name _____ **Date** _____

Level 2, Lesson 24

Review for Lessons 19-23

Follow along as your teacher reads each sentence. Write the Core Words in the correct blanks. Check your spelling.

_____   _____

1. Do you know _____ the _____ is?

                                                    _____

2. My grandfather rode a _____ and

   _____

   _____ to school.

                   _____ _____

3. I always _____ _____ my sister

   before school.

                                   _____

4. I don't know what that _____ is, but it is very

   _____

   _____ .

                           _____   _____

5. Bud swept _____ bit of _____ off

   the sidewalk.

Name _____ Date _____

Level 2, Lesson 24

Review for Lessons 19–23

Read each answer. Fill in the space in the Answer Rows for the choice that has a spelling error. If there is no mistake, fill in the last answer space.

1. A shaim
   B much
   C who
   D teach
   E (No mistake)

2. F maney
   G shore
   H bath
   J yard
   K (No mistake)

3. A shirt
   B verry
   C flash
   D with
   E (No mistake)

4. F farm
   G dirt
   H darc
   J what
   K (No mistake)

5. A peech
   B barn
   C horse
   D give
   E (No mistake)

6. F where
   G chick
   H shark
   J short
   K (No mistake)

7. A does
   B klash
   C tooth
   D park
   E (No mistake)

8. F first
   G live
   H shine
   J hoorn
   K (No mistake)

ANSWER ROWS
1. Ⓐ Ⓑ Ⓒ Ⓓ Ⓔ   3. Ⓐ Ⓑ Ⓒ Ⓓ Ⓔ   5. Ⓐ Ⓑ Ⓒ Ⓓ Ⓔ   7. Ⓐ Ⓑ Ⓒ Ⓓ Ⓔ
2. Ⓕ Ⓖ Ⓗ Ⓙ Ⓚ   4. Ⓕ Ⓖ Ⓗ Ⓙ Ⓚ   6. Ⓕ Ⓖ Ⓗ Ⓙ Ⓚ   8. Ⓕ Ⓖ Ⓗ Ⓙ Ⓚ

Lesson 24 Review 189

Name _____ Date _____

Level 2, Lesson 24
Review for Lessons 19–23

The Best School Show

Do you like school shows? What was the best school show you have ever gone to? What made it the best for you? Maybe you, a friend, or the whole school got an award. Use as many Core Words as you can.

Follow these steps:

1. Begin by explaining what you are writing about.

2. Explain why you remember this show. Why was it the best show you have ever gone to?

3. Tell whether you think you will ever go to another show as special as this one.

Remember...

• Take some time to plan.

• Write down any ideas you have on scrap paper.

• Write your paper.

• Look over your work. Check it for spelling and other mistakes. Fix any that you find.

Name _____ **Date** _____

Level 2, Lesson 24

Review for Lessons 19–23

Find the Core Word that is spelled correctly and fits best in the blank. Mark your answers in the Answer Rows.

1. Do you know _____ there is night?
   A why   B wy   C whye   D whie

2. It is important to _____ people for gifts.
   F thak   G thenk   H thank   J thanck

3. We watched the _____ swim in a pool at the zoo.
   A shrk   B sharc   C sherck   D shark

4. I think we should wash the dishes _____.
   F furst   G ferst   H first   J firs

5. This _____ will help you with your spelling.
   A thig   B thing   C theng   D thng

6. Kyle read _____ his sister drew.
   F wile   G whyle   H wyle   J while

7. Don't _____ the dog by putting its collar on too tight.
   A choke   B chok   C choak   D chocke

8. A wheel fell off the _____ on the way to town.
   F kart   G cartt   H cart   J cort

ANSWER ROWS
1. Ⓐ Ⓑ Ⓒ Ⓓ   3. Ⓐ Ⓑ Ⓒ Ⓓ   5. Ⓐ Ⓑ Ⓒ Ⓓ   7. Ⓐ Ⓑ Ⓒ Ⓓ
2. Ⓕ Ⓖ Ⓗ Ⓙ   4. Ⓕ Ⓖ Ⓗ Ⓙ   6. Ⓕ Ⓖ Ⓗ Ⓙ   8. Ⓕ Ⓖ Ⓗ Ⓙ

Name _____ **Date** _____

Level 2, Lesson 24

Review for Lessons 19-23

Find the underlined part of each sentence that is misspelled. If all the words are correct, choose <u>No mistake</u>. Mark your answers in the Answer Rows.

1. In <u>airt</u>, I painted a <u>girl</u> holding a <u>bird</u>.   <u>No mistake</u>.
      A   B   C   D

2. The <u>shark</u> has <u>very</u> <u>sharpe</u> teeth.   <u>No mistake</u>.
      F   G   H   J

3. I felt <u>shame</u> after I tried to feed the <u>horse</u> <u>dert</u>. <u>No mistake</u>.
      A   B C   D

4. My favorite <u>shirt</u> is too <u>shart</u>, so I will <u>give</u> it away.   <u>No mistake</u>.
                 F   G   H   J

5. <u>Whoo</u> <u>does</u> <u>more</u> work than I?   <u>No mistake</u>.
      A   B   C   D

6. If you <u>teach</u> me, I will <u>thank</u> you as long as I <u>live</u>. <u>No mistake</u>.
            F   G   H   J

7. I <u>couldn't</u> remember <u>whut</u> I did with my lost <u>tooth</u>. <u>No mistake</u>.
      A   B   C   D

8. We <u>wer</u> looking <u>for</u> the <u>first</u> star of the night.   <u>No mistake</u>.
      F   G   H   J

ANSWER ROWS 1. Ⓐ Ⓑ Ⓒ Ⓓ   3. Ⓐ Ⓑ Ⓒ Ⓓ   5. Ⓐ Ⓑ Ⓒ Ⓓ   7. Ⓐ Ⓑ Ⓒ Ⓓ
                    2. Ⓕ Ⓖ Ⓗ Ⓙ   4. Ⓕ Ⓖ Ⓗ Ⓙ   6. Ⓕ Ⓖ Ⓗ Ⓙ   8. Ⓕ Ⓖ Ⓗ Ⓙ

Name _____ **Date** _____

Level 2, Lesson 24

Review for Lessons 19–23

Read each phrase. Choose the phrase in which the underlined word is not spelled correctly. Mark your answers in the Answer Rows.

1. A by the <u>shoor</u>
   B tiger <u>shark</u>
   C <u>want to</u>
      <u>teach</u>
   D dig in the
      <u>dirt</u>

2. F <u>many</u> friends
   G <u>farm</u> the
      land
   H <u>shien</u> the
      light
   J blow the.
      <u>horn</u>

3. A <u>your</u> pencil
   B yellow <u>chik</u>
   C <u>where</u> in the
      world
   D come <u>with</u>
      me

4. F <u>dark</u> blue
   G <u>thing</u> of
      beauty
   H little <u>gerl</u>
   J back in a
      <u>flash</u>

5. A <u>much</u> more
   B <u>hord</u> job
   C flower <u>cart</u>
   D <u>for</u> you

6. F <u>giv</u> presents
   G <u>first</u> grade
   H <u>live</u> each
      day
   J <u>while</u> you
      wait

7. A <u>thin</u> line
   B <u>very</u> funny
   C play at the
      <u>parck</u>
   D got a <u>shock</u>

8. F ride a <u>hors</u>
   G <u>peach</u> pit
   H a red <u>barn</u>
   J <u>yard</u> sale

ANSWER ROWS   1. Ⓐ Ⓑ Ⓒ Ⓓ   3. Ⓐ Ⓑ Ⓒ Ⓓ   5. Ⓐ Ⓑ Ⓒ Ⓓ   7. Ⓐ Ⓑ Ⓒ Ⓓ

                  2. Ⓕ Ⓖ Ⓗ Ⓙ   4. Ⓕ Ⓖ Ⓗ Ⓙ   6. Ⓕ Ⓖ Ⓗ Ⓙ   8. Ⓕ Ⓖ Ⓗ Ⓙ

Name _____ Date _____

Level 2, Lesson 24

Review for Lessons 19-23

Read each phrase. Choose the phrase in which the underlined word is not spelled correctly for the way it is used in the phrase. Mark your answers in the Answer Rows.

1. A <u>shark</u> tank
   B eat <u>for</u> apples
   C for <u>shame</u>
   D <u>choke</u> on food

2. F <u>your</u> coming
   G <u>sharp</u> scissors
   H <u>thank</u> you
   J a <u>short</u> time

3. A <u>who</u> knows
   B ask <u>why</u>
   C build a <u>shock</u>
   D button your <u>shirt</u>

4. F <u>every</u> day
   G colors <u>clash</u>
   H <u>thin</u> about it
   J <u>what</u> kind

5. A <u>bath</u> towel
   B pretty <u>bird</u>
   C <u>art</u> book
   D <u>barn</u> the wood

6. F <u>does</u> sit-ups
   G <u>liver</u> long
   H <u>peach</u> pie
   J front <u>yard</u>

7. A <u>more</u> help
   B <u>were</u> here
   C wash the <u>dirt</u> coat
   D <u>tooth</u> fairy

8. F fill out a <u>farm</u>
   G <u>horse</u> blanket
   H <u>park</u> the car
   J <u>very</u> fine

ANSWER ROWS   1. Ⓐ ⒷⒸⒹ   3. ⒶⒷⒸⒹ   5. ⒶⒷⒸⒹ   7. ⒶⒷⒸⒹ
              2. ⒻⒼⒽⒿ   4. ⒻⒼⒽⒿ   6. ⒻⒼⒽⒿ   8. ⒻⒼⒽⒿ

Name _____ **Date** _____

Level 2, Lesson 24

Review for Lessons 19–23

Use the following Core Words from Lessons 19–23 to complete this puzzle.

Lesson 19
where
shame

Lesson 20
with

Lesson 21
park
hard
cart
sharp
art

Lesson 22
dirt

Lesson 23
does
were
every
thing
your
give

ACROSS
1. What is in your garden
4. All
6. Please _____ it to me.
8. Not soft but _____
10. A sorry feeling
11. A grocery _____
12. A green place for fun
14. Come _____ me.

DOWN
2. Rhymes with *ring*
3. We _____ not ready.
5. Is this _____ hat?
7. Question word about a place
9. I do; he _____
10. The knife has a _____ point.
13. Crayons and paint are tools for this

Name _____ **Date** _____

Level 2, Lesson 25

Words with *br*, *fr*, and *tr*

Fold the paper in half. Use the blanks to write each word as it is read to you. Then, unfold the paper and correct any mistakes. Practice these words.

1. _____	1. *brag*
2. _____	2. *trade*
3. _____	3. *brick*
4. _____	4. *frisky*
5. _____	5. *train*
6. _____	6. *frog*
7. _____	7. *trick*
8. _____	8. *broom*
9. _____	9. *free*
10. _____	10. *bright*

Name _____ **Date** _____

Level 2, Lesson 25

Words with *br, fr,* and *tr*

Follow along as your teacher reads each sentence. Write the Core Words in the correct blanks. Check your spelling.

1. It's not nice to _____ that you rode with

   the _____ engineer.

2. _____ your fish for my _____.

3. I use a _____ to sweep the leaves from

   every _____ on the ground.

4. The _____ puppy played outside in the

   _____ sunlight.

5. The magician taught us a _____ for

   _____!

Name _____ Date _____

Level 2, Lesson 25

Words with *br*, *fr*, and *tr*

Words can have more than one meaning. Sometimes a word can be both a noun and a verb. Read each sentence. Write *noun* or *verb* to show how the underlined word is used in the sentence. Use your Speller Dictionary to check your answers.

CORE WORDS

brag
trade
brick
frisky
train
frog
trick
broom
free
bright

1. We can take a <u>train</u> to the city. _____

2. I will <u>train</u> my dog. _____

3. Would you like to <u>trade</u> sandwiches? _____

4. That sports card was a good <u>trade</u>. _____

5. Clyde will <u>trick</u> his sister into giving him her markers. _____

6. Did you perform the <u>trick</u> that made the rabbit appear? _____

Name _____ Date _____

Level 2, Lesson 25

Words with *br*, *fr*, and *tr*

PUZZLE

Read each clue. Write the correct Core Word in the puzzle. Use the word list to help you.

CORE WORDS

Across

2. A sweeper
4. Boast
7. Exchange
8. Lively

Down

1. Shiny
3. At no cost
4. Building material
5. Engine
6. Joke
8. Like a toad

brag
trade
brick
frisky
train
frog
trick
broom
free
bright

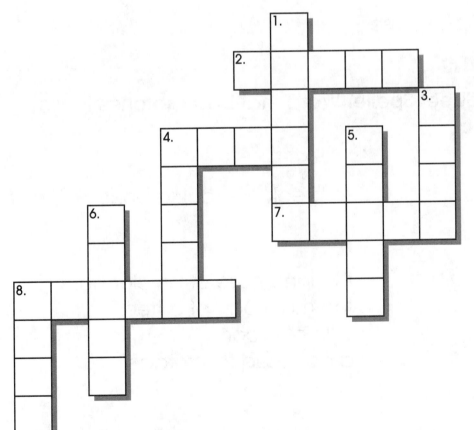

Name _____ Date _____

Level 2, Lesson 25

Words with *br*, *fr*, and *tr*

SUPER SPELLER WORDS

trunk   bruise   fracture

LETTER CLUES

Write the missing letters in the
Super Speller Words. Then write the word.

1. _____ _____unk   _____

2. _____ _____acture   _____

3. _____ _____uise   _____

DEFINITIONS

Write the Super Speller Word that best matches these
definitions.

4. _____ : to break or crack a bone

5. _____ : the long nose of an elephant
                         : the main part of a tree
                         : part of a car
                         : a box used for storage

Name _____ Date _____

Level 2, Lesson 25

Words with *br*, *fr*, and *tr*

CROSS-CURRICULAR WORDS

bran   **frost**   **trait**

WORD SORT

Write the Cross-Curricular Word that matches each spelling pattern below.

fr	br	tr
1. _____	2. _____	3. _____

WORD BUILDING

Cross out the endings of the words below to make Cross-Curricular Words.

4. branch _____   6. frosted _____

5. traitor _____

RHYMING WORDS

Write the Cross-Curricular Word that rhymes with each word below.

7. lost _____   9. bait _____

8. ran _____

Name _____ Date _____

Level 2, Lesson 25

Words with *br*, *fr*, and *tr*

Read the story. Find 8 misspellings and 4 other mistakes in the story. Use all 3 proofreading marks to correct the story. Write the misspelled words correctly on the lines.

Proofreading Marks					
⬭	misspelling	=	make a capital letter	⊙	add a period

CORE WORDS

brag
trade
brick
frisky
train
frog
trick
broom
free
bright

One brit morning, Brad and fran went outside.

"I don't want to brage," said Brad, "but you should see my frog My forg can do a trick. It can hop over a brik and a brom."

"Can it hop over a tran?" asked Fran

"Oh no, it's not that friksy!" Brad said.

"Do you want to traid your frog?" asked Fran.

"Only if you let me play with it," he said

1. _____ 5. _____

2. _____ 6. _____

3. _____ 7. _____

4. _____ 8. _____

Name _____ Date _____

Level 2, Lesson 25

Words with *br*, *fr*, and *tr*

CORE WORDS

brag	brick	train	trick	free
trade	frisky	frog	broom	bright

Here is some information about pronouns:

Pronouns can take the place of nouns. When you use a pronoun, you have to know for whom or what the pronoun stands.

Clyde is my friend. **He** lives next door.

Read the sentences. Underline the pronoun. Draw an arrow to the noun for which it stands.

1. Rascal is a male dog. He is frisky.

2. Look at the frog. It jumped!

3. Do you know Therese? She lives in the brick house.

4. Christa and George walk to school. They do this every morning.

Complete each sentence with a pronoun.

5. Mario says _____ uses a broom to sweep.

6. Carla likes to brag that _____ can do a cartwheel.

Name _____ **Date** _____

Level 2, Lesson 26

Words with *sl* and *sp*

Fold the paper in half. Use the blanks to write each word as it is read to you. Then, unfold the paper and correct any mistakes. Practice these words.

1. _____	1.	*slam*
2. _____	2.	*speed*
3. _____	3.	*slip*
4. _____	4.	*spin*
5. _____	5.	*sled*
6. _____	6.	*space*
7. _____	7.	*slide*
8. _____	8.	*speech*
9. _____	9.	*slick*
10. _____	10.	*spy*

Name _____ **Date** _____

Level 2, Lesson 26

Words with *sl* and *sp*

Follow along as your teacher reads each sentence. Write the Core Words in the correct blanks. Check your spelling.

1. Be careful you don't _____ on the _____ ice!

2. Does Earth really _____ around in _____?

3. We used my red _____ to _____ down the hill.

4. We saw the baseball _____ through the air and _____ into a window!

5. She gave a _____ about her adventures as a _____.

Name _____ **Date** _____

Level 2, Lesson 26

Words with *sl* and *sp*

Words are in ABC order in a dictionary. If the first letters are the same, look at the second letters. If the second letters are the same, look at the third letters, and so on. When the letters are different, you use them to put the words in ABC order.

CORE WORDS

slam
speed
slip
spin
sled
space
slide
speech
slick
spy

Write the Core Words in the order you would find them in a dictionary.

1. _____ 6. _____

2. _____ 7. _____

3. _____ 8. _____

4. _____ 9. _____

5. _____ 10. _____

Name _____ **Date** _____

Level 2, Lesson 26

Words with *sl* and *sp*

CONTEXT CLUES

Use Core Words to finish the signs.

Be careful on hill
_____
----
1. _____

will pick up
_____

2. _____

The ice is
_____
----
5. _____

you might
_____

----
6. _____

or
_____

7. _____

CORE WORDS

slam
speed
slip
spin
sled
space
slide
speech
slick
spy

No
cars in
this
_____
----
3. _____

Come to hear the
_____
----
8. _____

today

Do not
_____
----
4. _____

this door

Tops that
_____
----
9. _____

are sold here

Name _____ **Date** _____

Level 2, Lesson 26

Words with *sl* and *sp*

SUPER SPELLER WORDS

slender   sprain   slimy

WORD SORT

Write the Super Speller Word that starts with *sp.*

1. _____

Write the Super Speller Words that start with *sl.*

2. _____

3. _____

WORD PARTS

Write the Super Speller Words that have the following smaller words in them.

4. rain _____

5. lend _____

6. slim _____

Name _____ **Date** _____

Level 2, Lesson 26

Words with *sl* and *sp*

CROSS-CURRICULAR WORDS

slime
slate
spice

LETTER CLUES

Write the missing letters to complete each
Cross-Curricular Word.

_____ _____

1. _____ _____ice

2. _____ _____ate

3. _____ _____ime

SYNONYMS

Write the Cross-Curricular Word that means nearly the
same as each word below.

4. seasoning _____

5. rock _____

6. muck _____

Name _____ Date _____

Level 2, Lesson 26

Words with *sl* and *sp*

Read the story. Find 8 misspellings and 4 other mistakes in the story. Use all 3 proofreading marks to correct the story. Write the misspelled words correctly on the lines.

Proofreading Marks					
⬭	misspelling	＝	make a capital letter	⊙	add a period

CORE WORDS

slam
speed
slip
spin
sled
space
slide
speech
slick
spy

I'm going to the lake to skate. the ice is thick and slikk We need to be careful not to slep. there is enough spasse on the ice for everyone. when skaters spen, space is important. If you want to make a spech, watch out for spinning skaters! Look at that spead skater go! She is crouched down like a spy. Some children slidde down the big hill. Then they pull their slad back to the top.

1. _____

2. _____

3. _____

4. _____

5. _____

6. _____

7. _____

8. _____

Name _____ **Date** _____

Level 2, Lesson 26

Words with *sl* and *sp*

CORE WORDS

slam	slip	sled	slide	slick
speed	spin	space	speech	spy

A sentence has a subject and a verb.

1. If the subject is about one thing, it is singular. Use a singular verb. *The girl reads a book.*
   Subject Verb

2. If the subject is about more than one thing, it is plural. Use a plural verb. *The girls read a book.*
   Subject Verb

Write the correct verb on the line.

1. Scott (slam/slams) _____ the door.

2. The seals (slip/slips) _____ on the ice.

3. We (slide/slides) _____ across the floor.

4. The clothes (spin/spins) _____ in the dryer.

5. I (spy/spies) _____ a spider on the wall.

6. The train (speed/speeds) _____ away.

Name _____ **Date** _____

Level 2, Lesson 27
Words with -s

Fold the paper in half. Use the blanks to write each word as it is read to you. Then, unfold the paper and correct any mistakes. Practice these words.

1. _____
2. _____
3. _____
4. _____
5. _____
6. _____
7. _____
8. _____
9. _____
10. _____

1. *animals*
2. *ants*
3. *chickens*
4. *seals*
5. *cows*
6. *ducks*
7. *rabbits*
8. *snakes*
9. *whales*
10. *zebras*

Name _____ **Date** _____

Level 2, Lesson 27

Words with -s

Follow along as your teacher reads each
sentence. Write the Core Words in the
correct blanks. Check your spelling.

1. The striped _____ are my favorite

   _____ in the zoo.

2. The _____ are very small, and the

   _____ are very big!

3. The _____ cluck and the

   _____ moo.

4. The _____ and _____ swim.

5. Both furry _____ and scaly

   _____ go underground.

Name _____ **Date** _____

Level 2, Lesson 27

Words with -s

If you wanted to look up *ducks* in a dictionary, you would look up the word *duck*. If a word has an ending, look up the word without the ending. What words would you look up in the dictionary to find the meanings of these words?

CORE WORDS

animals
ants
chickens
seals
cows
ducks
rabbits
snakes
whales
zebras

1. chickens _____

2. snakes _____

3. animals _____

4. zebras _____

5. ants _____

6. seals _____

7. whales _____

8. cows _____

Name _____ **Date** _____

Level 2, Lesson 27
Words with -s
PUZZLE

Follow the path from the inside of the snail shell to the outside. Find five Core Words. Circle each letter.

CORE WORDS

animals
ants
chickens
seals
cows
ducks
rabbits
snakes
whales
zebras

LETTER SCRAMBLE

Unscramble the underlined Core Word in each sentence. Write it on the line.

1. Can <u>sleas</u> play horns? _____

2. <u>Zbasre</u> are black and white. _____

3. <u>Skanse</u> do not feel slimy. _____

4. I have two pet <u>bbarits</u>. _____

Name _____ Date _____

Level 2, Lesson 27

Words with -s

SUPER SPELLER WORDS

boards   potatoes   suspenders

CLASSIFYING

Write the Super Speller Word that best goes with each group.

1. beans, rice, _____

2. pants, shirt, _____

3. hammer, nails, _____

PLURALS

Write the singular form of each Super Speller Word.

4. boards _____

5. potatoes _____

LETTER SCRAMBLE

Circle the hidden Super Speller Word.

6. jkuiolsuspendersletuiju   8. potpeteboardsacky

7. boadspotatoeskullp

Name _____ **Date** _____

Level 2, Lesson 27

Words with -*s*

CROSS-CURRICULAR WORDS

lizards   **ladybugs**   **grasshoppers**

PLURALS

Write the word that shows the singular form of each Cross-Curricular Word below.

1. lizards _____

2. ladybugs _____

3. grasshoppers _____

CONTEXT CLUES

Write Cross-Curricular Words to complete the story.

Richie went to the pet store to buy two scaly,

spiny 4. _____. The pet store owner sold

him a bag of green 5. _____ to feed

them. On the way home, three red 6. _____

flew onto Richie's hand.

Name _____ **Date** _____

Level 2, Lesson 27

Words with -s

Read the story. Find 7 misspellings and 4 other mistakes in the story. Use all 3 proofreading marks to correct the story. Write the misspelled words correctly on the lines.

Proofreading Marks					
⬭	misspelling	=	make a capital letter	⊙	add a period

CORE WORDS

animals
ants
chickens
seals
cows
ducks
rabbits
snakes
whales
zebras

This park has all kinds of animels All over the animal park there are antz looking for food They are even in the cage with the rabits. In one part of the park are lions, bears, and zebas. There are snackes, too. some animal parks have whaales, but this one does not. Before i go home I always stop to see the seels.

1. _____

2. _____

3. _____

4. _____

5. _____

6. _____

7. _____

Name _____ Date _____

Level 2, Lesson 27

Words with -s

CORE WORDS

animals	chickens	cows	rabbits	whales
ants	seals	ducks	snakes	zebras

Here is some information about prepositions:

1. Most prepositions tell when or where.

2. Some prepositions are *above, after, at, before, below, by, down, during, for, from, in, into, on, over, through, under, up,* and *with.*

Underline the preposition and the phrase connected to it.

1. The farmer looked for the animals.

2. The children ran after the ducks.

3. The elephants ate before the zebras.

4. Can you swim with the whales?

5. The lettuce is hidden under the rabbits.

6. The stripes on the snakes are red.

7. A flower is blooming by the ants.

8. The eggs are from the chickens.

9. Birds fly over the cows every morning.

Name _____ **Date** _____

Level 2, Lesson 28

Words That Sound Alike

Fold the paper in half. Use the blanks to write each word as it is read to you. Then, unfold the paper and correct any mistakes. Practice these words for the final test.

1. _____	1.	*see*
2. _____	2.	*road*
3. _____	3.	*meet*
4. _____	4.	*deer*
5. _____	5.	*die*
6. _____	6.	*meat*
7. _____	7.	*sea*
8. _____	8.	*dear*
9. _____	9.	*dye*
10. _____	10.	*rode*

Name _____ **Date** _____

Level 2, Lesson 28

Words That Sound Alike

Follow along as your teacher reads each sentence. Write the Core Words in the correct blanks. Check your spelling.

1. You can't _____ very far down that dark

   _____

   _____.

2. They may _____ a shy _____

   in the forest.

3. I won't let this plant _____ because it is

   very _____ to me.

4. We _____ to the store to get _____

   for the cookout.

5. I bought blue _____ to make my shirt

   the color of the _____.

Name _____ **Date** _____

Level 2, Lesson 28

Words That Sound Alike

Homophones are words that sound alike but have different spellings and meanings.

CORE WORDS

see
road
meet
deer
die
meat
sea
dear
dye
rode

Find the word that is not used correctly in each sentence. Then write the homophone for that word.

1. The cowgirl road on a horse.

   _____

   _____

2. Did you meat anyone new today?

   _____

   _____

3. I saw a dear leap through a field.

   _____

   _____

4. I can sea you perfectly well.

   _____

   _____

5. If the spiders dye we will remove the

   _____

   web. _____

Name _____ **Date** _____

Level 2, Lesson 28

Words That Sound Alike

CONTEXT CLUES

Use the pair of Core Words in the box to finish the name of each song. Begin each Core Word with a capital letter.

Road Rode

CORE WORDS

1. The _____ Is Long

   Where I _____ My Bike

see
road
meet
deer
die
meat
sea
dear
dye
rode

See Sea

2. _____ Where the

   _____ Breeze Blows

Deer Dear

3. Remember the _____ in

   the Forest, _____?

Name _____ Date _____

Level 2, Lesson 28

Words That Sound Alike

SUPER SPELLER WORDS

weigh   **bored**   **knew**

HOMOPHONES

Write the Super Speller Word that is a homophone of each word below.

1. board _____

2. new _____

3. way _____

LETTER CLUES

Write the missing letters in the Super Speller Words. Then write the words.

4. w_____ _____ _____ _____

5. _____new _____

6. bo_____ _____

Name _____ **Date** _____

Level 2, Lesson 28

Words That Sound Alike

CROSS-CURRICULAR WORDS

peak   poor   cent

HOMOPHONES

Write the Cross-Curricular Word that is the homophone of each word below.

1. sent _____

2. pour _____

3. peek _____

RHYMING WORDS

Write the Cross-Curricular Word that best completes each rhyme.

4. The money was sent, but I did not get one

_____

_____ !

5. I climbed and climbed to take a peek at the

_____

highest, coldest mountain _____ .

6. We were very _____ until from our faucet

gold began to pour.

Name _____ Date _____

Level 2, Lesson 28

Words That Sound Alike

Read the story. Find 7 misspellings and 4 other mistakes in the letter. Use all 3 proofreading marks to correct the letter. Write the misspelled words correctly on the lines.

Proofreading Marks					
⬭	misspelling	⸗	make a capital letter	⊙	add a period

CORE WORDS

see
road
meet
deer
die
meat
sea
dear
dye
rode

Late one night we raod home from town We stopped near the sae to watch the sun go down. it seemed to diy the sky bright red! As we drove, there was almost no one on the rood. suddenly, a dier ran across the road in front of us. I hoped it would not diy My dad told me I'll meit the deer again someday.

1. _____

2. _____

3. _____

4. _____

5. _____

6. _____

7. _____

Name _____ **Date** _____

Level 2, Lesson 28

Words That Sound Alike

CORE WORDS

see	meet	die	sea	dye
road	deer	meat	dear	rode

These verbs have an unusual past tense:

Present Tense	Past Tense
see	saw
ride	rode
meet	met
eat	ate

Complete each sentence pair with a verb from the chart.

1. Yesterday we _____ at the sea.

   Today we _____ at the sea.

2. Do you _____ the deer?

   We _____ the deer last night.

3. Did you _____ pie yesterday?

   We _____ pie.

Name _____ **Date** _____

Level 2, Lesson 29
Family Words

Fold the paper in half. Use the blanks to write each word as it is read to you. Then, unfold the paper and correct any mistakes. Practice these words for the final test.

1. _____	1. *mother*
2. _____	2. *family*
3. _____	3. *grandfather*
4. _____	4. *aunt*
5. _____	5. *brother*
6. _____	6. *grandmother*
7. _____	7. *baby*
8. _____	8. *sister*
9. _____	9. *uncle*
10. _____	10. *father*

Name _____ **Date** _____

Level 2, Lesson 29

Family Words

Follow along as your teacher reads each sentence. Write the Core Words in the correct blanks. Check your spelling.

1. My _____ and _____ are my

    parents.

2. I'm an only child, so I have no _____ or

    _____.

3. They have a newborn _____ in their

    _____.

4. I want to visit my _____ Sally, my

    _____ Max, and my cousins.

5. My _____ and _____ are both

    60 years old.

Name _____ Date _____

Level 2, Lesson 29

Family Words

What words would you look up in the dictionary to find the meanings of these words?

CORE WORDS

mother
family
grandfather
aunt
brother
grandmother
baby
sister
uncle
father

1. aunts _____

2. fathers _____

3. brothers _____

4. grandmothers _____

5. families _____

6. mothers _____

7. grandfathers _____

8. uncles _____

9. babies _____

10. sisters _____

Name _____   **Date** _____

Level 2, Lesson 29

Family Words

CLASSIFYING

Look at the title for each list. Write the Core Words that go in each list.

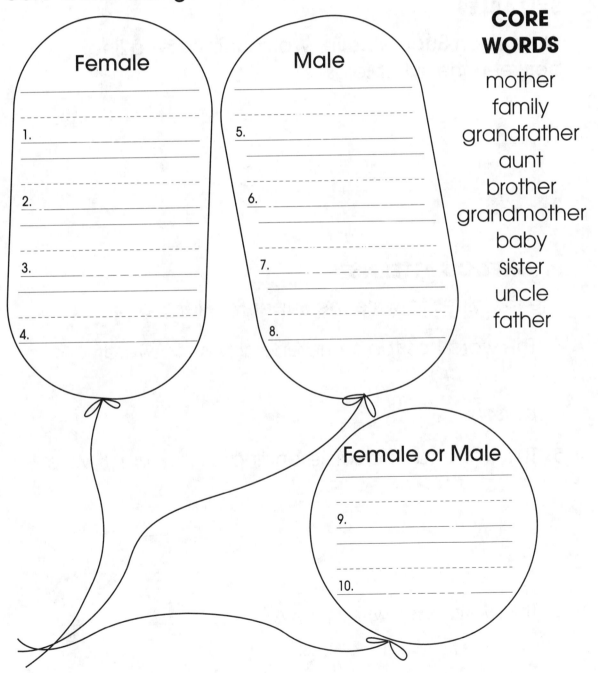

CORE WORDS

mother
family
grandfather
aunt
brother
grandmother
baby
sister
uncle
father

Female

1. _____
2. _____
3. _____
4. _____

Male

5. _____
6. _____
7. _____
8. _____

Female or Male

9. _____
10. _____

Name _____ Date _____

Level 2, Lesson 29

Family Words

SUPER SPELLER WORDS

granddaughter   **grandson**   **grandpa**

SYLLABLES

Write each Super Speller Word and draw a line between the syllables.

1. _____

2. _____

3. _____

PHONETIC PATTERNS

Use the clues to write the Super Speller Words.

4. This word has the same ending as the word _____ *person.* _____

5. This word has the same ending as the word *water.*
_____

6. This word ends with a vowel. _____

Name _____ **Date** _____

Level 2, Lesson 29

Family Words

CROSS-CURRICULAR WORDS

cousin   niece   nephew

LETTER CLUES

Write the missing letters to complete each
Cross-Curricular Word.

1. c_____ _____sin

2. n_____ _____ce

3. ne_____ _____ew

RIDDLES

Write the Cross-Curricular Word that answers each riddle.

4. I am the son of your brother. I am your

_____.

5. I am your aunt's daughter. I am your

_____.

6. I am your sister's daughter. I am your

_____.

Name _____ **Date** _____

Level 2, Lesson 29
Family Words

Read the story. Find 8 misspellings and 4 other mistakes in the story. Use all 3 proofreading marks to correct the story. Write the misspelled words correctly on the lines.

Proofreading Marks					
◯	misspelling	=	make a capital letter	⊙	add a period

CORE WORDS

mother
family
grandfather
aunt
brother
grandmother
baby
sister
uncle
father

We had a famly party last week My moter and father made the food My mother invited her mother, my grandmother. My farthar invited his father, my grandfarther My father also invited my uncil. my mother's sistr came. She is my favorite aent. She brought her son, Roberto, and her babee girl, Felicia.

1. _____

2. _____

3. _____

4. _____

5. _____

6. _____

7. _____

8. _____

Name _____ Date _____

Level 2, Lesson 29

Family Words

CORE WORDS

mother   grandfather   brother   baby   uncle
family   aunt   grandmother   sister   father

Here is some information about plurals:

You can make most nouns mean more than
one by adding **-s** or **-es** to the end of the word.
This is called a plural noun.

Write each of the following Core Words to mean "more
than one."

1. mother _____

2. father _____

3. sister _____

4. brother _____

5. grandmother _____

6. aunt _____

Name _____

Date _____

Level 2, Lesson 30

Review for Lessons 25–29

Fold the paper in half. Use the blanks to write each word as it is read to you. Then, unfold the paper and correct any mistakes. Practice these words.

1. _____	1. *train*
2. _____	2. *slip*
3. _____	3. *animals*
4. _____	4. *deer*
5. _____	5. *grandmother*
6. _____	6. *bright*
7. _____	7. *speech*
8. _____	8. *snakes*
9. _____	9. *sea*
10. _____	10. *sister*

Name _____ **Date** _____

Level 2, Lesson 30

Review for Lessons 25-29

Follow along as your teacher reads each sentence. Write the Core Words in the correct blanks. Check your spelling.

1. My _____ is not afraid of

   _____.

2. Did you hear the _____ my

   _____ gave?

3. The _____ sun shone on the calm

   _____.

4. Of all the forest _____, the _____

   is my favorite.

5. My toy _____ will not _____ off of

   the track.

Name _____ Date _____

Level 2, Lesson 30

Review for Lessons 25–29

Read each answer. Fill in the space in the Answer Rows for the choice that has a spelling error. If there is no mistake, fill in the last answer space.

1. A frisky
   B sled
   C ducks
   D sea
   E (No mistake)

2. F sisder
   G free
   H dear
   J animals
   K (No mistake)

3. A road
   B granfather
   C trick
   D space
   E (No mistake)

4. F rabbits
   G spiy
   H uncle
   J bright
   K (No mistake)

5. A slam
   B ants
   C mete
   D aunt
   E (No mistake)

6. F frog
   G slied
   H snakes
   J dye
   K (No mistake)

7. A father
   B brag
   C speed
   D chikens
   E (No mistake)

8. F deer
   G brother
   H trane
   J speech
   K (No mistake)

ANSWER ROWS
1. Ⓐ Ⓑ Ⓒ Ⓓ Ⓔ   3. Ⓐ Ⓑ Ⓒ Ⓓ Ⓔ   5. Ⓐ Ⓑ Ⓒ Ⓓ Ⓔ   7. Ⓐ Ⓑ Ⓒ Ⓓ Ⓔ
2. Ⓕ Ⓖ Ⓗ Ⓙ Ⓚ   4. Ⓕ Ⓖ Ⓗ Ⓙ Ⓚ   6. Ⓕ Ⓖ Ⓗ Ⓙ Ⓚ   8. Ⓕ Ⓖ Ⓗ Ⓙ Ⓚ

Name _____ **Date** _____

Level 2, Lesson 30

Review for Lessons 25-29

Favorite Animal

What is your favorite animal? Think about a pet you or a friend has. Maybe you saw the animal on a farm or zoo visit. Tell why others should also like this animal. Use as many Core Words as you can.

Follow these steps:

1. Begin by telling what your favorite animal is. Tell why you like this animal the best.

2. Write about what the animal looks like and how it acts.

3. Tell whether it lives in the water or on land. Does it live in warm or cold weather?

4. Then tell why you think this animal should be a favorite for other people, too.

Remember...

• Take some time to plan.

• Write down any ideas you have on scrap paper.

• Write your paper.

• Look over your work. Check it for spelling and other mistakes. Fix any that you find.

Name _____ **Date** _____

Level 2, Lesson 30

Review for Lessons 25-29

Find the Core Word that is spelled correctly and fits best in the blank. Mark your answers in the Answer Rows.

1. There are ten people in my _____.
   A family   B famley   C famely   D family

2. Ham is my favorite kind of _____.
   F mete   G meit   H meat   J met

3. The _____ were all sleeping in the barn.
   A anamals   B animals   C animalls   D anemils

4. Our _____ program is very interesting.
   F space   G spase   H spais   J spaise

5. Will you _____ me your pear for this apple?
   A traid   B traed   C trayd   D trade

6. My older _____ said I could not ride his bike.
   F bruther   G brothr   H brother   J brothir

7. I am raising _____ to show at the fair.
   A rabits   B rabets   C rabitts   D rabbits

8. The roads are _____ with ice.
   F slik   G slick   H sleck   J slic

ANSWER ROWS   1. Ⓐ Ⓑ Ⓒ Ⓓ   3. Ⓐ Ⓑ Ⓒ Ⓓ   5. Ⓐ Ⓑ Ⓒ Ⓓ   7. Ⓐ Ⓑ Ⓒ Ⓓ
   2. Ⓕ Ⓖ Ⓗ Ⓙ   4. Ⓕ Ⓖ Ⓗ Ⓙ   6. Ⓕ Ⓖ Ⓗ Ⓙ   8. Ⓕ Ⓖ Ⓗ Ⓙ

Name _____ Date _____

Level 2, Lesson 30

Review for Lessons 25–29

Find the underlined part of each sentence that is misspelled.
If all the words are correct, choose <u>No mistake</u>. Mark your
answers in the Answer Rows.

1. The <u>seals</u> didn't need a <u>slad</u> to <u>slide</u> down the hill. <u>No mistake</u>.
       A   **B**   **C**   **D**

2. My <u>aunt</u> would not let my <u>brother</u> cross the <u>roade</u>. <u>No mistake</u>.
      F   **G**   **H**   **J**

3. My <u>granmother</u> taught me a <u>slick</u> <u>trick</u>. <u>No mistake</u>.
       A   **B** **C**   **D**

4. At the zoo, they <u>train</u> killer <u>whales</u> to <u>spin</u> in the air. <u>No mistake</u>.
            F   **G**   **H**   **J**

5. In my <u>speech</u> about <u>animals</u>, I didn't mention <u>snaiks</u>. <u>No mistake</u>.
         A   **B**   **C**   **D**

6. The hungry <u>ducks</u> got a <u>frey</u> meal from the <u>sea</u>. <u>No mistake</u>.
          F   **G**   **H**   **J**

7. I'll <u>meet</u> my <u>family</u> at the <u>space</u> museum. <u>No mistake</u>.
      A   **B**   **C**   **D**

8. The croaking <u>frogg</u> will <u>slip</u> out of the <u>bright</u> sun. <u>No mistake</u>.
          F   **G**   **H**   **J**

ANSWER ROWS   1. Ⓐ Ⓑ Ⓒ Ⓓ   3. Ⓐ Ⓑ Ⓒ Ⓓ   5. Ⓐ Ⓑ Ⓒ Ⓓ   7. Ⓐ Ⓑ Ⓒ Ⓓ
                    2. Ⓕ Ⓖ Ⓗ Ⓙ   4. Ⓕ Ⓖ Ⓗ Ⓙ   6. Ⓕ Ⓖ Ⓗ Ⓙ   8. Ⓕ Ⓖ Ⓗ Ⓙ

Name _____ Date _____

Level 2, Lesson 30

Review for Lessons 25-29

Read each phrase. Choose the phrase in which the underlined word is not spelled correctly. Mark your answers in the Answer Rows.

1. A <u>bragg</u> about
   B wild <u>animals</u>
   C <u>slam</u> the door
   D <u>trade</u> seats

2. F <u>ants</u> in your pants
   G <u>family</u> photo
   H cross the <u>road</u>
   J <u>scee</u> a problem

3. A <u>brick</u> wall
   B my favorite <u>aunt</u>
   C Bill's <u>mather</u>
   D <u>train</u> tracks

4. F <u>sled</u> dog
   G <u>spead</u> up
   H milk <u>cows</u>
   J the plant may <u>die</u>

5. A <u>spen</u> the top
   B tree <u>frog</u>
   C older <u>brother</u>
   D leave some <u>space</u>

6. F red <u>meat</u>
   G help my <u>grandmother</u>
   H trained <u>seels</u>
   J dirty <u>trick</u>

7. A playground <u>slide</u>
   B <u>deere</u> crossing
   C cottontail <u>rabbits</u>
   D rolling <u>sea</u>

8. F newborn <u>baby</u>
   G famous <u>speech</u>
   H straw <u>broom</u>
   J <u>duks</u> quack

ANSWER ROWS
1. (A)(B)(C)(D)   3. (A)(B)(C)(D)   5. (A)(B)(C)(D)   7. (A)(B)(C)(D)
2. (F)(G)(H)(J)   4. (F)(G)(H)(J)   6. (F)(G)(H)(J)   8. (F)(G)(H)(J)

242 Lesson 30 Review

Name _____ **Date** _____

Level 2, Lesson 30

Review for Lessons 25–29

Read each phrase. Choose the phrase in which the underlined word is not spelled correctly for the way it is used in the phrase. Mark your answers in the Answer Rows.

1. A <u>slip</u> and fall
   B <u>meat</u> me at school
   C feed the <u>chickens</u>
   D nice to <u>meet</u> you

2. F fire <u>aunt</u>
   G <u>frisky</u> puppy
   H <u>grandfather</u> clock
   J youngest <u>sister</u>

3. A <u>free</u> samples
   B oil <u>slick</u>
   C filled to the <u>broom</u>
   D humpback <u>whales</u>

4. F blue <u>dye</u>
   G <u>spy</u> on you
   H <u>bright</u> colors
   J <u>cows</u> an accident

5. A <u>speech</u> loudly
   B my <u>grandmother</u> made
   C ask your <u>mother</u>
   D <u>zebras</u> at the zoo

6. F <u>see</u> the sunrise
   G down the <u>road</u>
   H white-tailed <u>dear</u>
   J grand <u>slam</u>

7. A watch out for <u>deer</u>
   B my <u>ants</u>, Mary and Jane
   C <u>trade</u> secrets
   D <u>speed</u> limit

8. F flock of <u>ducks</u>
   G bring your <u>sled</u>
   H <u>slide</u> down
   J <u>die</u> the fabric

ANSWER ROWS
1. Ⓐ Ⓑ Ⓒ Ⓓ
2. Ⓕ Ⓖ Ⓗ Ⓙ
3. Ⓐ Ⓑ Ⓒ Ⓓ
4. Ⓕ Ⓖ Ⓗ Ⓙ
5. Ⓐ Ⓑ Ⓒ Ⓓ
6. Ⓕ Ⓖ Ⓗ Ⓙ
7. Ⓐ Ⓑ Ⓒ Ⓓ
8. Ⓕ Ⓖ Ⓗ Ⓙ

Name _____ Date _____

Level 2, Lesson 30

Review for Lessons 25–29

Use the following Core Words from Lessons 25–29 to complete this puzzle.

Lesson 25
train
bright
frisky

Lesson 26
speech
slip

Lesson 27
animals
snakes

Lesson 28
deer
die
meat
sea
rode

Lesson 29
baby
sister
grandmother

ACROSS
3. He _____ his bike.
4. The light is _____.
6. Rhymes with *brain*
9. A plant without water will do this
10. Birds, fish, cows
12. Food from animals
13. Young child
14. Not a brother, a _____
15. _____ and slide

DOWN
1. The president gave a _____.
2. A male _____ has antlers.
5. Your mother's mother
7. Bouncy and playful
8. Ocean
11. Reptiles without arms or legs

Name _____ **Date** _____

Level 2, Lesson 31

The /o͝o/ Sound

Fold the paper in half. Use the blanks to write each word as it is read to you. Then, unfold the paper and correct any mistakes. Practice these words.

#		#	
1.	_____	1.	*book*
2.	_____	2.	*push*
3.	_____	3.	*took*
4.	_____	4.	*full*
5.	_____	5.	*foot*
6.	_____	6.	*bush*
7.	_____	7.	*hook*
8.	_____	8.	*pull*
9.	_____	9.	*wool*
10.	_____	10.	*good*

Name _____ Date _____

Level 2, Lesson 31
The /o͝o/ Sound
Follow along as your teacher reads each sentence. Write the Core Words in the correct blanks. Check your spelling.

_____   _____

1. Is that _____ a _____ one

   to read?

   _____   _____

2. I have to _____ my _____

   down into my boot.

   _____

3. Who _____ my coat off the

   _____

   _____ where it was hanging?

   _____

4. The sheep had a _____ coat of

   _____

   _____.

   _____

5. Help me _____ these berries off the

   _____

   _____.

Name _____ **Date** _____

Level 2, Lesson 31
The /o͝o/ Sound

Look at the entry for *push*.

push /po͝osh/ *verb* **pushed, pushing.**
1. to press on something in order to move it.
I pushed the cart through the market.
2. to move forward with effort. *We had to push
through the crowd.*

**CORE
WORDS**

book
push
took
full
foot
bush
hook
pull
wool
good

Use the entry for push to answer the
questions below.

1. How many definitions are there
   for *push*?

   _____

   _____

2. What is the second definition for *push*?

   _____

   _____

   _____

   _____

3. What is the sample sentence for the
   first meaning of *push*?

   _____

   _____

   _____

   _____

Name _____ **Date** _____

Level 2, Lesson 31

The /o͝o/ Sound

PUZZLE

Use Core Words to complete the puzzle.

Across

2. Opposite of bad
4. Opposite of empty
5. A shrub
7. Hang something on this
8. Past tense of *take*

Down

1. Comes from sheep
3. Hold and move forward
5. You read this
6. You hop on this

CORE WORDS

book
push
took
full
foot
bush
hook
pull
wool
good

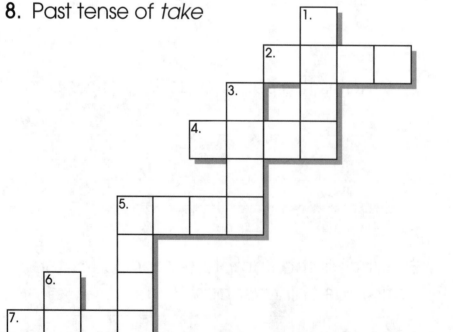

What Core Word is the opposite
_____
of 3 Down? _____

Name _____ Date _____

Level 2, Lesson 31

The /ŏŏ/ Sound

SUPER SPELLER WORDS

footman
bookmaker
bookkeeper

PHONETIC PATTERNS

Write the Super Speller Words in alphabetical order.
Then circle the /ŏŏ/ sound in each word.

1. _____   3. _____

2. _____

DEFINITIONS

Each of the Super Speller Words names a job. Write the
Super Speller Word that best completes each definition.

4. The _____ keeps track of a

company's money.

5. A _____ is a kind of servant.

6. A _____ makes books.

Name _____ Date _____

Level 2, Lesson 31
The /o͝o/ Sound
CROSS-CURRICULAR WORDS

wood
wolf
bull

WORD BUILDING

Solve the word problems to write the Cross-Curricular Words.

1. wolves - ves + f = _____

2. bulletin - etin = _____

3. hardwood - hard = _____

CLASSIFYING

Write the Cross-Curricular Word that belongs with each pair of words below.

4. tree, lumber, _____

5. wild, dog, _____

6. male, cow, _____

Name _____ **Date** _____

Level 2, Lesson 31

The /o͝o/ Sound

Read the story. Find 8 misspellings and 5 other mistakes in the story. Use all 3 proofreading marks to correct the story. Write the misspelled words correctly on the lines.

Proofreading Marks					
⬭	misspelling	≡	make a capital letter	⊙	add a period

my mom tuk me fishing. She showed me how to put bait on my hok. She put some red wul on my hook for the fish to see. i tried to put my line in the water, but it got caught in a buch. I couldn't puch the bush away I had to tug to poll it free my mom pulled in lots of fish. I stood on one fot and then the other, waiting for fish to bite. We left with a pail foll of fish.

CORE WORDS

book
push
took
full
foot
bush
hook
pull
wool
good

1. _____

2. _____

3. _____

4. _____

5. _____

6. _____

7. _____

8. _____

Name _____ **Date** _____

Level 2, Lesson 31
The /ŏŏ/ Sound

CORE WORDS

book	took	foot	hook	wool
push	full	bush	pull	good

To make a contraction you:

leave out the **o** in *not* and put an apostrophe (') in its place.

is not = isn't   *was not = wasn't*

are not = aren't   *were not = weren't*

Rewrite the underlined words as contractions.

1. This <u>is not</u> a hook. _____

2. We <u>were not</u> full from the snack. _____

3. The bush <u>was not</u> green. _____

4. They <u>are not</u> going to pull the wagon. _____

5. My foot <u>is not</u> big. _____

Name _____ **Date** _____

Level 2, Lesson 32

Words with *-ed* or *-ing*

Fold the paper in half. Use the blanks to write each word as it is read to you. Then, unfold the paper and correct any mistakes. Practice these words.

1. _____	1.	*bat*
2. _____	2.	*mop*
3. _____	3.	*tapped*
4. _____	4.	*cutting*
5. _____	5.	*hit*
6. _____	6.	*tap*
7. _____	7.	*batting*
8. _____	8.	*mopped*
9. _____	9.	*hitting*
10. _____	10.	*cut*

Name _____ Date _____

Level 2, Lesson 32

Words with *-ed* or *-ing*

Follow along as your teacher reads each sentence. Write the Core Words in the correct blanks. Check your spelling.

_____ _____

1. I took my baseball _____ to _____

   practice.

   _____

2. Mom gave me a _____ and we

   _____

   _____ the dirty floor.

   _____

3. The barber is _____ Dad's hair, then she'll

   _____

   _____ mine.

   _____

4. "Help me _____ on the window," Charlie

   _____

   said as he _____.

   _____

5. "I see you are _____ better," said Mom

   _____

   as I _____ the ball.

Name _____ **Date** _____

Level 2, Lesson 32

Words with *-ed* or *-ing*

An entry word is the word you look up in the dictionary. The way the word is said comes after the entry. Then the part of speech label is given. Different forms of the word appear after the part of speech label. Many entry words have more than one meaning. Look up the word *bat* in your Speller Dictionary to answer the questions.

CORE WORDS

bat
mop
tapped
cutting
hit
tap
batting
mopped
hitting
cut

1. How is the entry written to show how it is said?

   _____

   _____

2. What part of speech label appears for the second meaning for *bat*?

   _____

   _____

3. How many labels for parts of speech are there for the word *bat*?

   _____

   _____

Name _____ **Date** _____

Level 2, Lesson 32

Words with *-ed* or *-ing*

LETTER SCRAMBLE

Unscramble the underlined words. Use the Core Word list to help you.

1. Don't <u>apt</u> on the glass. _____

2. Who is first at <u>tab</u>? _____

3. I had to <u>mpo</u> the floor after the party. _____

4. I <u>patpde</u> my foot to the music. _____

5. We spent the day <u>cngiutt</u> out decorations. _____

6. The carpenter kept <u>gnhitit</u> his thumb with the hammer. _____

CORE WORDS

bat
mop
tapped
cutting
hit
tap
batting
mopped
hitting
cut

Name _____ **Date** _____

Level 2, Lesson 32

Words with *-ed* or *-ing*

SUPER SPELLER WORDS

printing   tiptoed   demanding

BASE WORDS

Write the base word of each Super Speller Word.

1. demanding _____

2. printing _____

3. tiptoed _____

WORD ENDINGS

Change the tense of each Super Speller Word. If the word ends in *-ing*, change the ending to *-ed* to make it past tense. If the word ends in *-ed*, change the ending to *-ing* to make it present tense.

4. demanding _____

5. tiptoed _____

6. printing _____

Name _____ Date _____

Level 2, Lesson 32
Words with *-ed* or *-ing*
CROSS-CURRICULAR WORDS
trap   trot   drop

WORD ENDINGS

Add the correct ending to each Cross-Curricular Word to make them past tense. Write the whole word on the line.

1. trap _____

2. trot _____

3. drop _____

CLASSIFYING

Think about whether each Cross-Curricular Word describes something done on land, in water, or both. Then write the words in the correct column.

Land	Water
4. _____	_____
5. _____	_____
6. _____	_____

Name _____ Date _____

Level 2, Lesson 32

Words with *-ed* or *-ing*

Read the story. Find 8 misspellings and 4 other mistakes in the story. Use all 3 proofreading marks to correct the story. Write the misspelled words correctly on the lines.

Proofreading Marks					
⬭	misspelling	≡	make a capital letter	⊙	add a period

"Can you bate that ball harder?" meghan asked

"I am bating it hard!" Pat told her.

"Can't you hitt it harder?"

"I'm hiting as hard as I can," he said.

"We don't have time to practice. we have to mope the floors before the game. This floor has not been moped in days!"

"don't tappe it, hit it hard!" she yelled. "If you don't, the coach will be cotting you from the team."

CORE WORDS

bat
mop
tapped
cutting
hit
tap
batting
mopped
hitting
cut

1. _____

2. _____

3. _____

4. _____

5. _____

6. _____

7. _____

8. _____

Name _____ **Date** _____

Level 2, Lesson 32
Words with *-ed* or *-ing*
CORE WORDS

bat	tapped	hit	batting	hitting
mop	cutting	tap	mopped	cut

Here are some facts about verbs and endings:

1. To make a verb tell about the past, add *-ed* to the end.

2. If the verb ends in **e**, just add *-d*.

3. Verbs that tell what one subject is doing end in *-s*.

Write the correct word to complete each sentence.

1. She (like/likes) _____ cutting the paper.

2. The ball player (bat/bats) _____ well.

3. They (hit/hits) _____ the ball.

4. We mopped and (clean/cleaned) _____ .

5. The players (like/likes) _____ hitting balls.

Name _____ **Date** _____

Level 2, Lesson 33

The /ou/ Sound

Fold the paper in half. Use the blanks to write each word as it is read to you. Then, unfold the paper and correct any mistakes. Practice these words.

1. _____	1. _____ *now*
2. _____	2. _____ *loud*
3. _____	3. _____ *down*
4. _____	4. _____ *house*
5. _____	5. _____ *clown*
6. _____	6. _____ *out*
7. _____	7. _____ *owl*
8. _____	8. _____ *sound*
9. _____	9. _____ *town*
10. _____	10. _____ *ouch*

Name _____ Date _____

Level 2, Lesson 33

The /ou/ Sound

Follow along as your teacher reads each sentence. Write the Core Words in the correct blanks. Check your spelling.

1. Listen to the happy _____ when the

   band comes into _____.

2. That silly _____ is much too

   _____.

3. I said "_____" after I fell _____.

4. "I'm going _____!" she said as she left

   the _____.

5. "It's night," said the _____, "so long for

   _____!"

Name _____ **Date** _____

Level 2, Lesson 33

The /ou/ Sound

Write each group of words in ABC order.
Remember to look at the second letters.

CORE WORDS

now
loud
down
house
clown
out
owl
sound
town
ouch

owl, out, down

1. _____

2. _____

3. _____

now, sound, loud

4. _____

5. _____

6. _____

owl, ouch, house

7. _____

8. _____

9. _____

loud, town, clown

10. _____

11. _____

12. _____

Name _____ Date _____

Level 2, Lesson 33

The /ou/ Sound
CONTEXT CLUES

Write a Core Word to finish each newspaper headline. Begin each Core Word with a capital letter.

1. Circus Is Coming to _____

2. _____ Rocket Blasts Off!

3. Car Runs _____ of Gas

4. Circus _____ Runs for Mayor

CORE WORDS

now
loud
down
house
clown
out
owl
sound
town
ouch

Write a rhyming Core Word in place of each underlined word.

5. If you bump your head you might say _____

"grouch." _____

6. *At the present time* means "wow." _____

7. The howl is a bird that flies and hunts. _____

_____

Name _____ **Date** _____

Level 2, Lesson 33
The /ou/ Sound
SUPER SPELLER WORDS

foul
stout
snout

LETTER CLUES

Write the missing letters in each of the Super Speller Words. Then write the words.

1. sn_____ _____t _____

2. f_____ _____l _____

3. st_____ _____t _____

ANTONYMS

Write the Super Speller Words that mean the opposite of the following words.

4. clean _____

5. thin _____

Name _____ Date _____

Level 2, Lesson 33

The /ou/ Sound

CROSS-CURRICULAR WORDS

route   underground railroad
tower

WORD SORT

Write the Cross-Curricular Word or term that matches each spelling pattern.

ou	**ow**
1. _____	3. _____
2. _____	

SYLLABLES

Write each Cross-Curricular Word or phrase and draw lines between the syllables.

4. _____	6. _____
5. _____	

RHYMING WORDS

Write the Cross-Curricular Word that rhymes with each word below.

7. shout _____   8. flower _____

Name _____ Date _____

Level 2, Lesson 33

The /ou/ Sound

Read the story. Find 8 misspellings and 4 other mistakes in the story. Use all 3 proofreading marks to correct the story. Write the misspelled words correctly on the lines.

Proofreading Marks					
⬭	misspelling	＝	make a capital letter	⊙	add a period

I heard a scary sound in my hous when my mother was owt. She went to toun while i was at home with my brother I looked around my house to see what the sownd could be. i thought it might be an oul. I looked doun the stairs, but there was nothing. I bumped into the door and said, "Ouch!" I heard my brother yell. "are you all right, you cloun?" Then the sound stopped. Nou I will never know what it was!

CORE WORDS

now
loud
down
house
clown
out
owl
sound
town
ouch

1. _____

2. _____

3. _____

4. _____

5. _____

6. _____

7. _____

8. _____

Name _____ **Date** _____

Level 2, Lesson 33

The /ou/ Sound

CORE WORDS

| now | down | clown | owl | town |
| loud | house | out | sound | ouch |

Here is some information about pronouns:

1. The word *I* is a pronoun.

2. When you talk about yourself in a sentence, use the word *me*.

3. The word *me* is a pronoun.

Complete each sentence with *I* or *me*.

1. _____ will read this book now.

2. Do you want to go to town with _____?

3. _____ like to read out loud.

4. Gracie and _____ saw an owl.

5. The teacher told Alex and _____ to not make a sound.

Name _____ **Date** _____

Level 2, Lesson 34

Compound Words

Fold the paper in half. Use the blanks to write each word as it is read to you. Then, unfold the paper and correct any mistakes. Practice these words.

1. _____	1. *maybe*
2. _____	2. *bedroom*
3. _____	3. *lunchroom*
4. _____	4. *notebook*
5. _____	5. *doghouse*
6. _____	6. *something*
7. _____	7. *myself*
8. _____	8. *nobody*
9. _____	9. *into*
10. _____	10. *inside*

Name _____ **Date** _____

Level 2, Lesson 34

Compound Words

Follow along as your teacher reads each sentence. Write the Core Words in the correct blank. Check your spelling.

1. Do you think _____ I left my _____ at home?

2. The baby fell asleep, so Dad carried her _____ _____ her _____ .

3. It's 12:00, but _____ is in the _____!

4. My dog sleeps _____ his _____.

5. This is _____ I want to do by _____ .

Name _____ **Date** _____

Level 2, Lesson 34

Compound Words

Some dictionary entries include example sentences. These sentences help explain the meaning of the entry words.

CORE WORDS

maybe
bedroom
lunchroom
notebook
doghouse
something
myself
nobody
into
inside

Write an example sentence of your own for four Core Words. Use your Speller Dictionary for help with the word meanings.

1. _____
_____
_____

2. _____
_____
_____

3. _____
_____
_____

4. _____
_____
_____

Name _____ **Date** _____

Level 2, Lesson 34

Compound Words

WORD BUILDING

Find two words in each sentence that make one Core Word. Write the word on the line.

1. I will eat my lunch in the room today.

   _____

   _____

2. Did you find a note in your spelling

   _____

   ----

   book? _____

3. My dog likes to stay in its own house at

   _____

   ----

   night. _____

4. Make the bed in your room before

   _____

   ----

   you leave. _____

5. There are no bones in the body of a

   _____

   ----

   worm. _____

6. Take the box in the kitchen to the

   _____

   ----

   shed. _____

CORE WORDS

maybe
bedroom
lunchroom
notebook
doghouse
something
myself
nobody
into
inside

Name _____ **Date** _____

Level 2, Lesson 34

Compound Words

SUPER SPELLER WORDS

briefcase   sunflower   spotlight

WORD PARTS

Divide each Super Speller Word into two smaller words.

1. spotlight   _____   _____

2. briefcase   _____   _____

3. sunflower   _____   _____

CONTEXT CLUES

Write the Core Word that best completes each sentence.

4. Peter has a beautiful _____ garden.

5. My mother carries her important papers in a

   _____

   _____ .

6. The singer stood in the _____ and sang.

Name _____ Date _____

Level 2, Lesson 34

Compound Words

CROSS-CURRICULAR WORDS

rockslide   landfill   thundercloud

WORD PARTS

Write the two words that make up each
Cross-Curricular Word.

1. thundercloud _____ _____

2. rockslide _____ _____

3. landfill _____ _____

WORD BUILDING

These word parts are out of order. Start with the first
word. Join the correct word parts to write the
Cross-Curricular Words.

rock   fill   4. _____

land   cloud   5. _____

thunder   slide   6. _____

Name _____ **Date** _____

Level 2, Lesson 34

Compound Words

Read the story. Find 8 misspellings and 4 other mistakes in the story. Use all 3 proofreading marks to correct the story. Write the misspelled words correctly on the lines.

Proofreading Marks					
⬭	misspelling	＝	make a capital letter	⊙	add a period

I couldn't find my notebok. I thought i left it in my bedrum, but it wasn't there I looked inside my house for it. I even checked the doghows. I knew that nobuddy else would want my notebook.

"don't worry," I told miself, "I'll find it."

The next day I went back to the lunchrum. I was a little nervous about walking intoo that big room. Then I saw someting on the table It was my notebook!

CORE WORDS

maybe
bedroom
lunchroom
notebook
doghouse
something
myself
nobody
into
inside

1. _____

2. _____

3. _____

4. _____

5. _____

6. _____

7. _____

8. _____

Name _____ Date _____

Level 2, Lesson 34
Compound Words

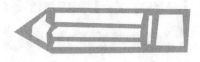

CORE WORDS

maybe	lunchroom	doghouse	myself	into
bedroom	notebook	something	nobody	inside

Remember to always capitalize:

1. the days of the week.

2. the months of the year.

Here is a "to do" list. Find words that should begin with a capital letter. Write the capital letter above the small letter. Then circle the Core Words.

1. On monday, clean my bedroom.

2. By april, build a doghouse for the puppy.

3. Buy a new notebook on saturday.

4. Read to myself for an hour every night in march.

5. Nobody allowed in my bedroom on thursday night.

6. Bring apple to lunchroom every friday.

7. Maybe visit Hallie on sunday.

8. Clean inside of garage with Dad in may.

Name _____ **Date** _____

Level 2, Lesson 35
Number Words

Fold the paper in half. Use the blanks to write each word as it is read to you. Then, unfold the paper and correct any mistakes. Practice these words.

1. _____	1. *one*
2. _____	2. *two*
3. _____	3. *three*
4. _____	4. *four*
5. _____	5. *five*
6. _____	6. *six*
7. _____	7. *seven*
8. _____	8. *eight*
9. _____	9. *nine*
10. _____	10. *ten*

Name _____ **Date** _____

Level 2, Lesson 35
Number Words

Follow along as your teacher reads each sentence. Write the Core Words in the correct blanks. Check your spelling.

_____ _____

1. We like to play "_____, _____,

   buckle my shoe."

2. I know what comes next, "_____,

   _____, shut the door!"

3. You have _____ fingers on each hand,

   or _____ fingers in all.

4. The word _____ rhymes with *sticks,* and

   _____ rhymes with *heaven.*

5. The word _____ rhymes with *late,* and

   _____ rhymes with *line.*

Name _____ **Date** _____

Level 2, Lesson 35

Number Words

Write the answer to each question. Use the dictionary entry for *one*.

CORE WORDS

one
two
three
four
five
six
seven
eight
nine
ten

one /wun/ *noun* **1.** the number 1. **2.** a single person or thing. *Pick the one you like best.* **3.** a person who stands for people in general. *One must try hard.*

1. What is the entry word?

_____

- -

_____

2. How many meanings does it have?

_____

- -

_____

3. Would the word *open* come before or after this word in the dictionary?

_____

- -

_____

4. Write a sample sentence for the first meaning of *one*.

_____

- -

_____

_____

- -

_____

Name _____ Date _____

Level 2, Lesson 35
Number Words
PUZZLE

Write the missing Core Words in the puzzle.
Each word is a name for a number.

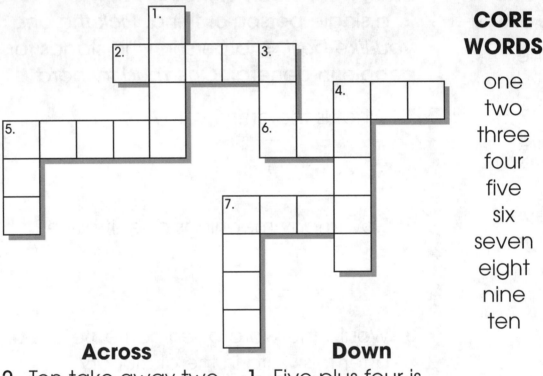

CORE WORDS

one
two
three
four
five
six
seven
eight
nine
ten

Across

2. Ten take away two is _____.
4. Ten take away four is _____.
5. Two plus one is _____.
6. How many dots does an *i* have?
7. The number that rhymes with *dive*

Down

1. Five plus four is _____.
3. The number of ears on a rabbit
4. Five apples plus two apples is _____.
5. The number after nine is _____.
7. How many children are there when there are two boys and two girls?

Name _____ Date _____

Level 2, Lesson 35
Number Words
SUPER SPELLER WORDS

forty   eighty   seventy

SYLLABLES

Write the Super Speller Words from least to greatest.
Then draw a line between each syllable.

1. _____

2. _____

3. _____

RIDDLES

Write the Super Speller Word that best answers each riddle.

4. I'm more than thirty, but less than fifty. What number

   am I? _____

5. I'm less than eighty, but more than sixty. What

   number am I? _____

6. I'm more than seventy, but less than ninety. What

   number am I? _____

Name _____ Date _____

Level 2, Lesson 35
Number Words
CROSS-CURRICULAR WORDS

ninety   fifty   thirty

PHONETIC PATTERNS

Write the Cross-Curricular Word that has the /ī/ sound.

1. _____

Write the Cross-Curricular Word that has the /i/ sound.

2. _____

Write the Cross-Curricular Word that has the same vowel sound as the word *bird.*

3. _____

RELATED WORDS

Write the Cross-Curricular Word that belongs with each group of words.

4. three, thirteen, third, _____

5. ninth, nine, nineteen, _____

6. five, fifth, fifteen, _____

Name _____ Date _____

Level 2, Lesson 35

Number Words

Read the story. Find 8 misspellings and 4 other mistakes in the story. Use all 3 proofreading marks to correct the story. Write the misspelled words correctly on the lines.

Proofreading Marks					
⬭	misspelling	＝	make a capital letter	⊙	add a period

can you count from wun to ten? One, tou, and three are first Do you know that one plus two equals thre? Wouldn't you like to learn what comes next? next are for, five, and six. Six minus one is five. You won't make a mistake if you are careful. Then come sevin, eight, and nine Two fours are the same as eaght. Did you know that three threes equal nin? One more and you have tne!

CORE WORDS

one
two
three
four
five
six
seven
eight
nine
ten

1. _____   5. _____

2. _____   6. _____

3. _____   7. _____

4. _____   8. _____

Name _____ **Date** _____

Level 2, Lesson 35
Number Words

CORE WORDS

one	three	five	seven	nine
two	four	six	eight	ten

If you want to:

1. tell something in a sentence, end the sentence with a (.).

2. ask something in a sentence, end it with a (?).

3. give a command in a sentence, end it with a (.).

4. show surprise in a sentence, end it with an (!).

Read the sentences. Put either a period, question mark, or exclamation point at the end. Then circle the Core Words.

1. My dog has four claws on each paw

2. Can you see all nine players on the team

3. Wash those three cars

4. This is one of my favorite books

5. I can't believe he ate eight hamburgers

6. May I please borrow six cents

Name _____ **Date** _____

Level 2, Lesson 36

Review for Lessons 31–35

Fold the paper in half. Use the blanks to write each word as it is read to you. Then, unfold the paper and correct any mistakes. Practice these words.

1. _____	1. *one*
2. _____	2. *myself*
3. _____	3. *out*
4. _____	4. *bat*
5. _____	5. *good*
6. _____	6. *eight*
7. _____	7. *something*
8. _____	8. *clown*
9. _____	9. *cut*
10. _____	10. *foot*

Name _____ **Date** _____

Level 2, Lesson 36

Review for Lessons 31–35

Follow along as your teacher reads each sentence. Write the Core Words in the correct blanks. Check your spelling.

1. Be careful not to _____ your _____

   on that broken glass.

2. Elise can _____ the ball right _____

   of the field.

3. I gave _____ apple to Jeff and had none

   for _____ .

4. The _____ threw _____ into

   the crowd.

5. I felt _____ when our cat had a litter of

   _____ kittens.

Name _____ Date _____

Level 2, Lesson 36

Review for Lessons 31–35

Read each answer. Fill in the space in the Answer Rows for the choice that has a spelling error. If there is no mistake, fill in the last answer space.

1. A pull
   B hiting
   C loud
   D maybe
   E (No mistake)

5. A hit
   B out
   C myself
   D eight
   E (No mistake)

2. F twoo
   G took
   H cutting
   J clown
   K (No mistake)

6. F good
   G bat
   H owch
   J lunchroom
   K (No mistake)

3. A something
   B seven
   C woul
   D cut
   E (No mistake)

7. A four
   B nin
   C tap
   D owl
   E (No mistake)

4. F now
   G bedrom
   H three
   J full
   K (No mistake)

8. F nobodey
   G foot
   H book
   J mop
   K (No mistake)

ANSWER ROWS   1. Ⓐ Ⓑ Ⓒ Ⓓ Ⓔ   3. Ⓐ Ⓑ Ⓒ Ⓓ Ⓔ   5. Ⓐ Ⓑ Ⓒ Ⓓ Ⓔ   7. Ⓐ Ⓑ Ⓒ Ⓓ Ⓔ
                      2. Ⓕ Ⓖ Ⓗ Ⓙ Ⓚ   4. Ⓕ Ⓖ Ⓗ Ⓙ Ⓚ   6. Ⓕ Ⓖ Ⓗ Ⓙ Ⓚ   8. Ⓕ Ⓖ Ⓗ Ⓙ Ⓚ

Name _____ Date _____

Level 2, Lesson 36

Review for Lessons 31–35

Class Party

Your class is planning a party for the end of second grade. Some students want to go to the zoo. Others want to spend the day at a nearby park. First, decide if you would like to go to the zoo or the park. Then, write a paper telling how you feel. Use as many Core Words as you can.

Follow these steps:

1. Begin by telling where you think the class should go.

2. Give reasons for your feelings. Use examples of what the class could do at the zoo or at the park.

3. Then tell why you think your classmates should go to either the zoo or the park.

Remember...

• Take some time to plan.

• Write down any ideas you have on scrap paper.

• Write your paper.

• Look over your work. Check it for spelling and other mistakes. Fix any that you find.

Name _____ **Date** _____

Level 2, Lesson 36

Review for Lessons 31–35

Find the Core Word that is spelled correctly and fits best in the blank. Mark your answers in the Answer Rows.

1. Show me _____ fingers.
   A fiv   B five   C fiev   D fiyv

2. The play will take place in the _____.
   F lonchroom G lunchrom H lunchroom J luchroom

3. I want to go to _____ school someday.
   A klown   B cloun   C kloun   D clown

4. After Mr. Guess _____ the floor, he sat and rested.
   F moppd   G mopd   H mopped   J moped

5. Will you please _____ me on the swing?
   A push   B poosh   C pushe   D poush

6. We put _____ oranges in each bag.
   F sevin   G seven   H sevn   J sivin

7. There was _____ stuck in the door.
   A somthing B somethig C sumthing D something

8. Can you tell where that sad _____ is coming from?
   F sownd   G soud   H sound   J sond

ANSWER ROWS   1. Ⓐ Ⓑ Ⓒ Ⓓ   3. Ⓐ Ⓑ Ⓒ Ⓓ   5. Ⓐ Ⓑ Ⓒ Ⓓ   7. Ⓐ Ⓑ Ⓒ Ⓓ
              2. Ⓕ Ⓖ Ⓗ Ⓙ   4. Ⓕ Ⓖ Ⓗ Ⓙ   6. Ⓕ Ⓖ Ⓗ Ⓙ   8. Ⓕ Ⓖ Ⓗ Ⓙ

Name _____ Date _____

Level 2, Lesson 36

Review for Lessons 31–35

Find the underlined part of each sentence that is misspelled. If all the words are correct, choose <u>No mistake</u>. Mark your answers in the Answer Rows.

1. While I was <u>cutting</u> the <u>bush</u>, an <u>oul</u> flew by.   <u>No mistake</u>.
           A   B   C   D

2. I rode <u>intoo</u> <u>town</u> to get a <u>book</u> .   <u>No mistake</u>.
        F   G   H   J

3. <u>Maybe</u> I can earn <u>one</u> dollar if I <u>mop</u> the floor.   <u>No mistake</u>.
    A   B   C   D

4. If you are happy, <u>tap</u> your <u>foot</u> <u>sixs</u> times.   <u>No mistake</u>.
              F   G   H   J

5. I told <u>myself</u> that <u>nobody</u> wants my <u>noatbook</u>.   <u>No mistake</u>.
      A   B   C   D

6. Mitch brought his <u>goud</u> <u>bat</u> to <u>batting</u> practice.   <u>No mistake</u>.
                F   G   H   J

7. Angie saw <u>foor</u> wasps <u>inside</u> the <u>doghouse</u>.   <u>No mistake</u>.
          A   B   C   D

8. The <u>house</u> made a <u>sound</u> when I <u>tappd</u> the door.   <u>No mistake</u>.
      F   G   H   J

ANSWER ROWS   1. Ⓐ Ⓑ Ⓒ Ⓓ   3. Ⓐ Ⓑ Ⓒ Ⓓ   5. Ⓐ Ⓑ Ⓒ Ⓓ   7. Ⓐ Ⓑ Ⓒ Ⓓ
                      2. Ⓕ Ⓖ Ⓗ Ⓙ   4. Ⓕ Ⓖ Ⓗ Ⓙ   6. Ⓕ Ⓖ Ⓗ Ⓙ   8. F Ⓖ Ⓗ Ⓙ

290 Lesson 36 Review

Name _____ Date _____

Level 2, Lesson 36

Review for Lessons 31-35

Read each phrase. Choose the phrase in which the underlined word is not spelled correctly. Mark your answers in the Answer Rows.

1. A off the <u>hook</u>
   B brown <u>batt</u>
   C chapter <u>book</u>
   D <u>now</u> or later

2. F <u>maybee</u> you can
   G <u>push</u> the button
   H <u>one</u> star
   J <u>mop</u> the floor

3. A <u>bedroom</u> window
   B <u>down</u> the hill
   C <u>toock</u> turns
   D in the <u>lunchroom</u>

4. F <u>full</u> of water
   G <u>house</u> cat
   H <u>cutting</u> her hair
   J <u>lowd</u> crash

5. A <u>thre</u> girls
   B <u>foot</u> pedal
   C <u>four</u> birds
   D <u>clown</u> around

6. F <u>five</u> questions
   G build a <u>doghowse</u>
   H trim the <u>bush</u>
   J <u>tap</u> your feet

7. A fell <u>owt</u>
   B <u>six</u> words
   C <u>something</u> blue
   D <u>batting</u> practice

8. F hooting <u>owl</u>
   G did it <u>myself</u>
   H <u>het</u> the deck
   J <u>seven</u> letters

ANSWER ROWS 1. Ⓐ Ⓑ Ⓒ Ⓓ   3. Ⓐ Ⓑ Ⓒ Ⓓ   5. Ⓐ Ⓑ Ⓒ Ⓓ   7. Ⓐ Ⓑ Ⓒ Ⓓ
2. Ⓕ Ⓖ Ⓗ Ⓙ   4. Ⓕ Ⓖ Ⓗ Ⓙ   6. Ⓕ Ⓖ Ⓗ Ⓙ   8. Ⓕ Ⓖ Ⓗ Ⓙ

Name _____ Date _____

Level 2, Lesson 36

Review for Lessons 31–35

Read each phrase. Choose the phrase in which the underlined word is not spelled correctly for the way it is used in the phrase. Mark your answers in the Answer Rows.

1. A <u>hook</u> and ladder truck
   B <u>tapped</u> on the window
   C <u>two</u> boys
   D both <u>foot</u>

2. F <u>one</u> the game
   G hard <u>hitting</u>
   H <u>notebook</u> paper
   J small <u>town</u>

3. A <u>into</u> the room
   B watch a <u>tap</u>
   C <u>nine</u> ducks
   D <u>good</u> night

4. F yelled <u>ouch</u>
   G <u>cut</u> in half
   H <u>eight</u> lunch
   J <u>hit</u> the target

5. A turn off the <u>house</u>
   B <u>pull</u> tight
   C clean the <u>wool</u>
   D screech <u>owl</u>

6. F say <u>something</u>
   G <u>ten</u> o'clock
   H <u>nobody</u> there
   J <u>full</u> down

7. A <u>six</u> eggs
   B up to <u>bat</u>
   C Nick <u>myself</u>
   D not <u>now</u>

8. F funny <u>clown</u>
   G <u>four</u> all time
   H <u>loud</u> noise
   J wet <u>mop</u>

ANSWER ROWS
1. Ⓐ Ⓑ Ⓒ Ⓓ   3. Ⓐ Ⓑ Ⓒ Ⓓ   5. Ⓐ Ⓑ Ⓒ Ⓓ   7. Ⓐ Ⓑ Ⓒ Ⓓ
2. Ⓕ Ⓖ Ⓗ Ⓙ   4. Ⓕ Ⓖ Ⓗ Ⓙ   6. Ⓕ Ⓖ Ⓗ Ⓙ   8. Ⓕ Ⓖ Ⓗ Ⓙ

Name _____ Date _____

Level 2, Lesson 36

Review for Lessons 31–35

Use the following Core Words from Lessons 31–35 to complete this puzzle.

Lesson 31
full
foot
good

Lesson 32
mopped
cut
batting

Lesson 33
clown
house
town
now

Lesson 34
myself
something
maybe

Lesson 35
eight
ten

ACROSS
2. Circus performer
5. Swinging the bat
6. Right _____!
8. Thing not known
13. He _____ the floor.
14. Not empty

DOWN
1. Small city
2. Divide with a knife
3. Perhaps
4. Rhymes with *mouse*
7. This number rhymes with *late.*
9. My own self
10. After nine is _____.
11. We had a _____ time.
12. It has toes.

SRA Spelling Student Progress Chart

Name _____

Percent Correct

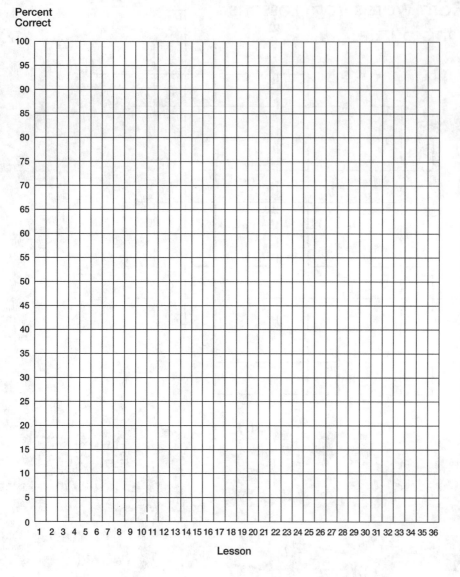

Percent
Correct

Lesson

Number Correct

	Pretest	Posttest
Lesson 1	_____	_____
Lesson 2	_____	_____
Lesson 3	_____	_____
Lesson 4	_____	_____
Lesson 5	_____	_____
Lesson 6	_____	_____
Lesson 7	_____	_____
Lesson 8	_____	_____
Lesson 9	_____	_____
Lesson 10	_____	_____
Lesson 11	_____	_____
Lesson 12	_____	_____
Lesson 13	_____	_____
Lesson 14	_____	_____
Lesson 15	_____	_____
Lesson 16	_____	_____
Lesson 17	_____	_____
Lesson 18	_____	_____
Lesson 19	_____	_____
Lesson 20	_____	_____
Lesson 21	_____	_____
Lesson 22	_____	_____
Lesson 23	_____	_____
Lesson 24	_____	_____
Lesson 25	_____	_____
Lesson 26	_____	_____
Lesson 27	_____	_____
Lesson 28	_____	_____
Lesson 29	_____	_____
Lesson 30	_____	_____
Lesson 31	_____	_____
Lesson 32	_____	_____
Lesson 33	_____	_____
Lesson 34	_____	_____
Lesson 35	_____	_____
Lesson 36	_____	_____

Dear Family,

This year, in addition to our work in other subject areas, we will be focusing on spelling, because we don't want to leave your child's success in writing and spelling to chance.

In first grade, your child should have learned that letters relate to sounds and that there are correct spellings for words. Words are spelled the same way every time they are written. In first grade, however, it is very common for children's primary spelling strategy to be spelling exactly what they hear. This results in some interesting but explainable spellings. For example:

BE PLIT. (Be polite.)

TCHR (Teacher)

This "phonemic" strategy builds the foundation for spelling, but it does not work for all words, since all words are not spelled as they sound. As children develop in spelling ability, they have to disassociate sound from spelling somewhat and learn spelling rules and patterns that include silent letters and endings for words. A "transitional" speller, for example, would spell the word *stopped* correctly, doubling the consonant and adding the ending. At an earlier stage, the child may have spelled the word STOPT, because that is the way it sounds.

Second graders exhibit different types of spelling ability. Many can spell a lot of words correctly. Some second graders still sound out every word. By looking carefully at your child's spellings, you can tell if he or she is developing spelling ability. In second grade, even though it is a misspelling, a good sign is when your child overgeneralizes a spelling rule or pattern and spells for example, EATTING for *eating*. This means that in addition to sounding the word out, he or she is beginning to apply spelling rules. You might want to keep a record of the more interesting spellings in your child's baby book, along with the first words he or she spoke.

You can help your children become competent spellers by encouraging them to read and write to help develop a visual memory of words. Don't hesitate to give a spelling if your child requests it.

Sincerely,

Dear Family,

In class we are continuing to focus on spelling. Each week we have a weekly word list. Each word on the word list follows a specific pattern, so that children learn that there are dependable spelling patterns they can rely on to spell a wide variety of words.

Research has shown that it takes several years for children to develop solid spelling skills. Unlike what many people think, most spellings are not learned by memorization. Instead children go through several stages of learning about letters, sounds, and the spelling patterns that make English spelling make sense. It takes the average child from three to six years to emerge as a fairly competent speller.

To help your child practice the weekly word list, say each word and make up a sentence to go with it. Have your child spell each word orally. If a mistake is made, have your child spell the word again, encouraging him or her to think about the spelling pattern. The next night, have your child write each word as you say it along with an example sentence. Check each word immediately after it is written. Give lavish praise for all words spelled correctly.

You should expect the words we have studied to be spelled correctly in writing. Many times, even when they know how to spell a word, children sound it out again. Sometimes this creates an error, especially in words like *said* or *you* that are not spelled the way they sound. If a mistake is made in a word that has been on a weekly word list, remind your child of the way it was spelled in the list and have him or her write the correct spelling.

Sincerely,

SRA
Spelling
Level 2 (English Spelling)

Dear Family,

In class we continue to focus on spelling. The children are developing a large bank of words they know how to spell. Along with sounding out words, they are demonstrating understanding of spelling patterns for word endings, silent letters, punctuation, and long vowel spellings.

Contrary to what many people think, English spelling does make sense. Many words are spelled the way they sound, but spelling is also organized by meaning patterns. Words that look the same usually have the same meaning root, although they may sound different. For example, *sign* is spelled with silent **g** because it is related in meaning to the words *signal* and *signature.* Letter placement is also an organizer for spelling. For example, no English words end in the letter **v.**

You can help your second grader by reading to your child and pointing out spellings of some of the familiar words. Encourage your child to keep a little notebook of words he or she can spell. This might include family names and the names of friends or pets. As time goes on, the list will become longer and longer, and you and your child can both be proud of what has been accomplished.

Sincerely,

Dear Family,

In class we are continuing to work on spelling. Through the weekly word lists, the children are developing a large list of high-frequency words they know how to spell.

Children learn to spell by learning spelling patterns and applying them in writing. The writing connection is very important. Many times, children spell words correctly on the weekly test and then misspell those same words in writing. This is because they are thinking of what their message is, rather than how to spell the word. This is appropriate for a first draft, but it is not appropriate for a final copy that other people will read. Misspelled words leave readers with a bad impression of the writer.

This is why, along with spelling, we also emphasize proofreading. Proofreading requires a lot of self-discipline. It requires the writer to read what he or she has written one more time before turning it in. These are the things a proofreader should check for:

- A clear message
- Proper punctuation
- Correct spelling

Encourage your child to write as much as possible. Here are some ideas:

- Make a list of things to do.
- Make a list of things to buy.
- Write a story.
- Write a letter to someone.
- Write a thank-you note.

After your child completes a piece of writing, have him or her read it and correct any mistakes. It is the final step, just like cleaning up after a meal.

Sincerely,

Level 2, Unit 1, Lesson 1
The /a/ Sound

CONTEXT SENTENCES POSTTEST
1. lap   map
2. pat   hat
3. man   jam
4. mad   ram
5. bad   gas

DICTIONARY ACTIVITY: ABC Order
1. c   6. w
2. f   7. cdef
3. a   8. nopq
4. n   9. lmno
5. s   10. hijk

HOME-STUDY ENRICHMENT ACTIVITY
Horizontal: hat, ram, jam, mad, lap
Vertical: man, bad, pat, map, gas

SUPER SPELLERS ACTIVITY
Phonetic Patterns
1. almond   3. jackal
2. jacket

Context Clues
4. jacket   6. jackal
5. almond

CROSS-CURRICULAR ACTIVITY:
Social Studies
Letter Clues
1. val   3. cac
2. a

Classifying
4. cactus   6. valley
5. tax

PROOFREADING ACTIVITY
Misspelled Core Words
1. jam   5. map
2. ram   6 man
3. gas   7. mad
4. lap   8. hat

Other Corrections
the man Lap. it was sad.

LANGUAGE ARTS ACTIVITY:
Capitalizing the First Word in a Sentence
1. The; Core Word: hat
2. Pat; Core Word: pat
3. Is; Core Word: gas
4. David; Core Word: man
5. Her; Core Word: lap

Level 2, Unit 1, Lesson 2
The /i/ Sound

CONTEXT SENTENCES POSTTEST
1. pin   if
2. his   zip
3. kiss   tip
4. milk   mix
5. fix   rip

DICTIONARY ACTIVITY: ABC Order
1. kiss   5. milk
2. his   6. rip
3. if   7. tip
4. rip   8. zip

HOME-STUDY ENRICHMENT ACTIVITY
1. mix   4. Pin
2. if   5. rip
3. fix   6. tip

SUPER SPELLERS ACTIVITY
Word Sort
1. twig   3. discover
2. mistakes

Word Parts
4. mistakes   6. discover
5. twig

CROSS-CURRICULAR ACTIVITY:
Math
Word Building
1. sixty
2. inch
3. number strip

Word Parts
4. sip, rip, tip, pit

PROOFREADING ACTIVITY
Misspelled Core Words
1. rip   5. zip
2. fix   6. mix
3. pin   7. kiss
4. tip   8. if

Other Corrections
zipper. he was   school. he will

LANGUAGE ARTS ACTIVITY: End Punctuation
1. .   5. ?
2. .   6. .
3. ?   7. !
4. !   8. .

Level 2, Unit 1, Lesson 3
The /o/ and /ô/ Sounds

CONTEXT SENTENCES POSTTEST
1. jog   log
2. flop   spot
3. fog   lot
4. got   cot
5. job   dog

DICTIONARY ACTIVITY: ABC Order
1. cot   5. lot
2. flop   6. spot
3. got   7. fog
4. dog

HOME-STUDY ENRICHMENT ACTIVITY
Context Clues
1. cot   4. jog
2. dog   5. fog
3. flop

SUPER SPELLERS ACTIVITY
Letter Clues
1. o   3. o
2. o

Riddles
4. bonnet   6. bottle
5. snort

CROSS-CURRICULAR ACTIVITY:
Science
Letter Clues
1. con   3. rock
2. os

Word Parts
4. contracts   6. rocket
5. ostrich

PROOFREADING ACTIVITY
Misspelled Core Words
1. got   5. jog
2. lot   6. log
3. dog   7. cot
4. spot   8. job

Other Corrections
job. It   my job   there is   tree. I

LANGUAGE ARTS ACTIVITY:
Quotation Marks in Dialogue
2. Alisha asked the nurse, "Should I stand on this spot?" Core Word: spot
3. "My dog will stay with you," Clyde said to Alisha. Core Word: dog
4. The nurse said, "You are all doing a fine job." Core Word: job
5. Alisha said, "I will have fun and flop on the cot." Core Words: flop, cot

Level 2, Unit 1, Lesson 4
The Final /k/ Sound

CONTEXT SENTENCES POSTTEST
1. stick   pack
2. snack   sack
3. lock   dock
4. kick   rock
5. sick   stack

DICTIONARY ACTIVITY: ABC Order
1. dock   5. rock
2. rock   6. stick
3. snack   7. b
4. kick

HOME-STUDY ENRICHMENT ACTIVITY
1. Rock   5. Kick
2. Dock   6. Sick
3. Sack   7. Stack
4. Lock

SUPER SPELLERS ACTIVITY
Phonetic Patterns
1. cloak   3. skunk
2. crock

Definitions
4. skunk   6. cloak
5. crock

CROSS-CURRICULAR ACTIVITY:
Science
Phonetic Patterns
1. tick   3. wick
2. track

Rhyming Words
4. tick   6. wick
5. track

PROOFREADING ACTIVITY
Misspelled Core Words
1. rock   5. stick
2. snack   6. lock
3. pack   7. dock
4. sack   8. kick

Other Corrections
nuts. put the   leave. later.

LANGUAGE ARTS ACTIVITY:
Commas in Friendly Letters
October 25, 1997 Dear Martha, Your good friend,

Core Words: dock, sick, lock, rock, kick, stack

Level 2, Unit 1, Lesson 5
The /nd/ and /st/ Sounds

CONTEXT SENTENCES POSTTEST

1. lost   pond
2. list   just
3. band   and
4. fast   last
5. hand   sand

DICTIONARY ACTIVITY: ABC Order

1. band   6. lost
2. last   7. fast
3. sand   8. hand
4. and   9. list
5. just   10. pond

HOME-STUDY ENRICHMENT ACTIVITY

Horizontal: list, pond, just, sand, and, last

Vertical: lost, fast, band, hand

SUPER SPELLERS ACTIVITY

Word Sort

1. stern   3. lend
2. strong

Letter Scramble

4. strong   6. lend
5. stern

CROSS-CURRICULAR ACTIVITY:
Science

Sort

1. expands   3. gust
2. frond

Synonyms

4. expands   6. frond
5. gust

PROOFREADING ACTIVITY

Misspelled Core Words

1. just   5. hand
2. pond   6. and
3. sand   7. last
4. fast   8. band

Other Corrections

we were   than i can   that was   saw her

LANGUAGE ARTS ACTIVITY:
Parentheses

1. (four of them); Core Word: band
2. (12.5 centimeters); Core Word: hand
3. (0.6 kilometers); Core Word: pond
4. (Students and Teachers); Core Word: and
5. (white and black sand); Core Words: sand, and
6. (lost and found); Core Words: lost, and
7. (3.2 kilometers); Core Word: last

Level 2, Unit 1, Lesson 6
Review Lessons 1-5

CONTEXT SENTENCES POSTTEST

1. band   if
2. stick   map
3. lock   gas
4. got   milk
5. flop   sand

STANDARDIZED-FORMAT TEST 1

1. a   5. b
2. h   6. h
3. b   7. a
4. j   8. k

PERFORMANCE ASSESSMENT
Students' writings will vary.

STANDARDIZED-FORMAT TEST 2

1. a   5. a
2. h   6. g
3. b   7. d
4. j   8. h

STANDARDIZED-FORMAT TEST 3

1. c   5. b
2. h   6. f
3. c   7. b
4. j   8. g

STANDARDIZED-FORMAT TEST 4

1. a   5. c
2. h   6. f
3. a   7. d
4. j   8. h

STANDARDIZED-FORMAT TEST 5

1. c   5. d
2. j   6. h
3. a   7. a
4. g   8. g

PUZZLE FUN

Across	Down
2. fog	1. rock
5. mix	2. fix
6. snack	3. gas
7. if	4. band
9. sand	5. milk
10. lock	8. flop
11. rip	9. stick
12. map	

Level 2, Unit 2, Lesson 7
The /e/ Sound

CONTEXT SENTENCES POSTTEST

1. went   egg
2. fed   nest
3. met   bend
4. yet   test
5. send   rest

DICTIONARY ACTIVITY: ABC Order

1. bend   6. rest
2. egg   7. send
3. fed   8. test
4. met   9. went
5. nest   10. yet

HOME-STUDY ENRICHMENT ACTIVITY

Letter Scramble

1. went   4. egg
2. send   5. nest
3. fed   6. bend

SUPER SPELLERS ACTIVITY

Syllables

1. he/li/cop/ter   3. res/cue
2. cel/ery

Classifying

4. celery   6. rescue
5. helicopter

CROSS-CURRICULAR ACTIVITY:
Math

Letter Clues

1. e   3. e
2. e

Context Clues

4. set   6. less than
5. twenty

PROOFREADING ACTIVITY

Misspelled Core Words

1. went   5. nest
2. met   6. rest
3. fed   7. yet
4. egg   8. send

Other Corrections

egg gate First most eggs I wrote

LANGUAGE ARTS ACTIVITY: Periods in Abbreviations

1. Rd.   3. St.
2. min.   4. Mr.

Level 2, Unit 2, Lesson 8
The /u/ Sound

CONTEXT SENTENCES POSTTEST

1. shut   rug
2. stuck   mud
3. tug   rust
4. must   us
5. rub   luck

DICTIONARY ACTIVITY: ABC Order

1. end   5. middle
2. middle   6. middle
3. end   7. end
4. end

HOME-STUDY ENRICHMENT ACTIVITY

Across	Down
2. rust	1. luck
3. stuck	3. shut
4. must	5. tug
6. us	

SUPER SPELLERS ACTIVITY

Letter Clues

1. u, plumber   3. u, stuffy
2. u, mustard

Letter Scramble

4. stuffy   6. mustard
5. plumber

CROSS-CURRICULAR ACTIVITY:
Math

Syllables

1. function   3. multiply
2. subtraction

Word Endings

4. function   5. subtraction

Related Words

6. subtraction   8. multiply
7. function

PROOFREADING ACTIVITY

Misspelled Core Words

1. must   5. rug
2. mud   6. stuck
3. rub   7. tug
4. rust   8. shut

Other Corrections

away my sister one tugg when we

LANGUAGE ARTS ACTIVITY:
Apostrophes in Possessives

1. Charlie's; Core Words: us, stuck, shut
2. sister's; Core Words: rub, rust
3. friend's; Core Word: must
4. girls'; Core Words: rug, mud

ANSWER KEY

Level 2, Unit 2, Lesson 9
Words with *gr*, *dr*, and *tr*

CONTEXT SENTENCES POSTTEST
1. drum   tree
2. drive   truck
3. trip   gray
4. drip   grin
5. grand   drove

DICTIONARY ACTIVITY: ABC Order
1. drip   6. gray
2. drive   7. grin
3. drove   8. tree
4. drum   9. trip
5. grand   10. truck

HOME-STUDY ENRICHMENT ACTIVITY

Horizontal: drive, drip, truck, grand, gray

Vertical: tree, drove, drum, trip, grin

SUPER SPELLERS ACTIVITY

Word Sort
1. dreadful   3. trying
2. grasp

Definitions
4. to hold firmly
5. frightening; very bad
6. making an effort

CROSS-CURRICULAR ACTIVITY: Social Studies

Word Parts
1. graph   3. dragon
2. truth

Rhyming Words
4. dragon

Plurals
5. dragon   7. graph
6. truth

PROOFREADING ACTIVITY

Misspelled Core Words
1. drive   5. tree
2. trip   6. drip
3. grin   7. gray
4. drove   8. grand

OTHER CORRECTIONS
Mom○ "where _it_ was window○We

LANGUAGE ARTS ACTIVITY: Kinds of Sentences
1. ?–Core Words: trip, gray
2. .–Core Words: drive, grand, tree
3. !–Core Word: grin
4. ?–Core Words: tree, truck
5. Sentences will vary; they end with a period.
6. Sentences will vary; they end with a question mark.

Level 2, Unit 2, Lesson 10
Words with *gl*, *bl*, and *pl*

CONTEXT SENTENCES POSTTEST
1. glad   blast
2. glass   plum
3. plan   plus
4. plot   blink
5. block   blend

DICTIONARY ACTIVITY: Entry Words
1. plot
2. an area of ground
3. The outlaws formed a plot to rob the stagecoach.
4. 2

HOME-STUDY ENRICHMENT ACTIVITY

Across	Down
2. glad	1. plan
3. blend	3. blink
4. block	4. blast
5. glass	6. plum
6. plot	
7. plus	

SUPER SPELLERS ACTIVITY

Letter Clues
1. g, l, glide   3. p, l, planetary
2. b, l, blinker

Word Building
4. glide   6. blinker
5. planetary

CROSS-CURRICULAR ACTIVITY: Science

Phonetic Patterns
1. glade   3. blood
2. plankton

Synonyms
4. plankton

PROOFREADING ACTIVITY

Misspelled Core Words
1. block   5. glass
2. plan   6. blend
3. blast   7. plot
4. blink   8. glad

Other Corrections
_we_ can an eye○ together○ block○

LANGUAGE ARTS ACTIVITY: Complete and Incomplete Sentences
1. x Core Words: block, glass
2. ✔Core Word: plum
3. ✔Core Word: blink
4. ✔Core Words: blast, plot
5. x Core Word: glad
6. x Core Word: blend
7. ✔Core Word: plus
8. ✔Core Word: plan

Level 2, Unit 2, Lesson 11
Words with *sk*, *mp*, and *ng*

CONTEXT SENTENCES POSTTEST
1. song   long
2. dump   camp
3. wing   sting
4. mask   desk
5. ask   jump

DICTIONARY ACTIVITY: ABC Order

Beginning: dump, desk

Middle: mask, long, jump

End: wing, sting

HOME-STUDY ENRICHMENT ACTIVITY
1. dump   4. desk
2. ask   5. mask
3. sting

SUPER SPELLERS ACTIVITY

Word Sort
1. cask   3. fling
2. lump

Synonyms
4. fling   6. cask
5. lump

CROSS-CURRICULAR ACTIVITY: Social Studies

Phonetic Patterns
1. stump   3. dusk
2. ring

Rhyming Words
4. dusk

PROOFREADING ACTIVITY

Misspelled Core Words
1. mask   5. dump
2. sting   6. long
3. camp   7. ask
4. desk   8. jump

Other Corrections
get a doo_r_○ _be_ careful _then_ you

LANGUAGE ARTS ACTIVITY: Compound Subjects and Verbs
1. The (desks and masks) are brown.
2. The (dump and the camp) have a sign in front of them.
3. The bug will (jump and sting) a smaller bug.
4. Children (read) first (and ask) questions later.

Level 2, Unit 2, Lesson 12
Review Lessons 7-11

CONTEXT SENTENCES POSTTEST
1. drive   shut
2. met   yet
3. grin   mask
4. mud   sting
5. blast   plus

STANDARDIZED-FORMAT TEST 1
1. a   5. b
2. k   6. f
3. a   7. d
4. h   8. k

PERFORMANCE ASSESSMENT
Students' writings will vary.

STANDARDIZED-FORMAT TEST 2
1. b   5. b
2. h   6. f
3. d   7. c
4. f   8. j

STANDARDIZED-FORMAT TEST 3
1. a   5. a
2. g   6. g
3. a   7. d
4. h   8. g

STANDARDIZED-FORMAT TEST 4
1. a   5. d
2. h   6. g
3. a   7. c
4. g   8. g

STANDARDIZED-FORMAT TEST 5

1. c   5. c
2. f   6. j
3. b   7. a
4. j   8. g

PUZZLE FUN

Across

3. mud
4. grin
5. us
7. sting
9. met
10. blast
11. glass
12. rest
13. bend

Down

1. drive
2. rust
3. must
6. plus
8. grand
9. mask

Level 2, Unit 3, Lesson 13
The /ā/ Sound

CONTEXT SENTENCES POSTTEST

1. came   cane
2. bait   pail
3. rake   hay
4. grape   plate
5. raise   say

DICTIONARY ACTIVITY: ABC Order

1. bait   6. pail
2. came   7. plate
3. cane   8. raise
4. grape   9. rake
5. hay   10. say

HOME-STUDY ENRICHMENT ACTIVITY

1. came, cane   3. grape, plate
2. raise, rake   4. say, hay

SUPER SPELLERS ACTIVITY

Phonetic Patterns

1. ai, rainbow   2. a, apron, acre

Letter Scramble

3. acre   5. apron
4. rainbow

CROSS-CURRICULAR ACTIVITY:
Social Studies

Word Sort

1. slavery   3. Spain
2. state

Word Parts

4. Spain   5. slavery

Definitions

6. state

PROOFREADING ACTIVITY

Misspelled Core Words

1. came   5. hay
2. say   6. bait
3. rake   7. cane
4. pail   8. grape

Other Corrections

i would   me˳ they would   grape˳

LANGUAGE ARTS ACTIVITY: Parts of a Sentence

1. pail/smells; Core Words: bait, pail
2. plate/holds; Core Words: plate, grape
3. rake/came; Core Words: rake, came
4. elephants/raise; Core Word: raise

Level 2, Unit 3, Lesson 14
The /ē/ Sound

CONTEXT SENTENCES POSTTEST

1. sheep   deep
2. each   meal
3. dream   bean
4. seen   wheel
5. treat   team

DICTIONARY ACTIVITY:
Pronunciation

1. team   5. deep
2. meal   6. dream
3. wheel   7. sheep
4. bean   8. seen

HOME-STUDY ENRICHMENT ACTIVITY

Horizontal: each, team, deep, treat, dream

Vertical: seen, wheel, bean, meal, sheep

SUPER SPELLERS ACTIVITY

Word Sort

1. sweet   3. reason
2. steed

Rhyming Words

4. steed   6. reason
5. sweet

CROSS-CURRICULAR ACTIVITY:
Social Studies

Word Sort

1. area   3. needs
2. key

Letter Clues

4. e   6. e
5. ee

Context Clues

7. area   8. key

PROOFREADING ACTIVITY

Misspelled Core Words

1. Each   5. treat
2. sheep   6. wheel
3. team   7. deep
4. meal   8. seen

Other Corrections

the cooks˳ do   treat˳

LANGUAGE ARTS ACTIVITY:
Possessive Nouns

1. the dream's beginning
2. the bean's seed
3. the wheel's center

Level 2, Unit 3, Lesson 15
The /ī/ Sound

CONTEXT SENTENCES POSTTEST

1. shy   pine
2. right   fight
3. light   wide
4. fly   dry
5. sight   night

DICTIONARY ACTIVITY: Multiple Meanings

1. shy   4. pine
2. light   5. fly
3. right

HOME-STUDY ENRICHMENT ACTIVITY

1. wide   6. dry
2. right   7. fly
3. sight   8. night
4. light   9. shy
5. pine   10. fight

SUPER SPELLERS ACTIVITY

Letter Clues

1. i, e   3. i, l, o
2. i, g, h

Context Clues

4. title   6. sigh
5. pilot

CROSS-CURRICULAR ACTIVITY:
Science

Phonetic Patterns

1. flight   5. flight
2. sky   6. vibrate
3. vibrate   7. sky
4. sky   8. flight

Synonyms

9. sky   11. flight
10. vibrate

PROOFREADING ACTIVITY

Misspelled Core Words

1. fly   5. dry
2. wide   6. fight
3. pine   7. night
4. light   8. sight

Other Corrections

we will   in the   city˳   site˳If

LANGUAGE ARTS ACTIVITY:
Possessive Pronouns

2. your sight
3. our night
4. The cat is hers.
5. The shy pet is mine.

Level 2, Unit 3, Lesson 16
The /ō/ Sound

CONTEXT SENTENCES POSTTEST

1. tow   boat
2. coat   snow
3. poke   goat/toad
4. blow   row
5. toad/goat   soap

DICTIONARY ACTIVITY: ABC Order

1. blow   6. row
2. boat   7. snow
3. coat   8. soap
4. goat   9. toad
5. poke   10. tow

HOME-STUDY ENRICHMENT ACTIVITY

Horizontal: snow, poke, boat, row, coat

Vertical: blow, soap, tow, goat, toad

SUPER SPELLERS ACTIVITY

Word Sort

1. bowl   3. oath
2. doze

Synonyms

4. oath   5. doze

Anagrams

6. bowl

CROSS-CURRICULAR ACTIVITY:
Science

Word Building
1. coal   3. echo
2. glow

Riddles
4. echo   6. glow
5. coal

PROOFREADING ACTIVITY

Misspelled Core Words
1. toad   5. row
2. soap   6. coat
3. boat   7. goat
4. snow   8. tow

Other Corrections
<u>s</u>he got <u>s</u>he began <u>s</u>he could goat_o

LANGUAGE ARTS ACTIVITY:
Comparisons
1. x   4. x
2. ✔   5. ✔
3. x   6. x

Level 2, Unit 3, Lesson 17
The /o͞o/ Sound

CONTEXT SENTENCES POSTTEST
1. tune   boot
2. moon   room
3. tube   pool
4. zoo   soon
5. rude   food

DICTIONARY ACTIVITY: Multiple
Meanings
1. b   3. a
2. a   4. b

HOME-STUDY ENRICHMENT
ACTIVITY
1. Pool   5. Room
2. Moon   6. Rude
3. Food   7. Tube
4. Zoo

SUPER SPELLERS ACTIVITY

Letter Clues
1. o, o, gloom   3. u, cruel
2. u, e, costume

Antonyms
4. gloom   5. cruel

CROSS-CURRICULAR ACTIVITY:
Math

Letter Clues
1. u   3. u
2. u

Phonetic Patterns
4. cube   6. rule
5. unit

Plurals
7. cubes   9. units
8. rules

PROOFREADING ACTIVITY

Misspelled Core Words
1. zoo   5. boot
2. food   6. tune
3. pool   7. moon
4. tube   8. soon

Other Corrections
<u>did</u> <u>s</u>he sends moon_o soon_o

LANGUAGE ARTS ACTIVITY:
Common Nouns
1. tune   7. tube
2. moon   8. room
3. pool   9. room, I, moon
4. zoo   10. seals, pool, zoo
5. boot   11. I, tune, tube
6. food

Level 2, Unit 3, Lesson 18
Review Lessons 13–17

CONTEXT SENTENCES POSTTEST
1. sheep   zoo
2. raise   light
3. blow   soap
4. sight   team
5. moon   plate

STANDARDIZED-FORMAT TEST 1
1. b   5. a
2. f   6. h
3. c   7. d
4. f   8. k

PERFORMANCE ASSESSMENT
Students' writings will vary.

STANDARDIZED-FORMAT TEST 2
1. d   5. d
2. g   6. h
3. a   7. a
4. h   8. g

STANDARDIZED-FORMAT TEST 3
1. d   5. c
2. f   6. g
3. b   7. a
4. f   8. h

STANDARDIZED-FORMAT TEST 4
1. b   5. d
2. f   6. h
3. c   7. b
4. g   8. j

STANDARDIZED-FORMAT TEST 5
1. b   5. b
2. f   6. f
3. c   7. d
4. j   8. f

PUZZLE FUN

Across	Down
1. plate	2. team
3. boat	3. blow
4. wide	5. dream
7. sheep	6. raise
9. sight	7. soap
10. moon	8. wheel
11. deep	9. snow
12. row	

Level 2, Unit 4, Lesson 19
Words with *wh* and *sh*

CONTEXT SENTENCES POSTTEST
1. what   shine
2. clash   where
3. flash   shock
4. while   shore
5. Why   shame

DICTIONARY ACTIVITY: Entry Words
1. shore   4. shame
2. 2   5. 2
3. land

HOME-STUDY ENRICHMENT
ACTIVITY
1. While   4. shoRe
2. wHy   5. shinE
3. shamE   6. where

SUPER SPELLERS ACTIVITY

Word Sort
1. shale   3. whisk
2. smallish

Definitions
4. shale   6. smallish
5. whisk

CROSS-CURRICULAR ACTIVITY:
Science

Classifying
1. showers   3. wheat
2. shone

Antonyms
4. Showers   5. shone

PROOFREADING ACTIVITY

Misspelled Core Words
1. shore   5. What
2. flash   6. shine
3. clash   7. while
4. shock   8. Why

Other Corrections
<u>s</u>heri sky_o <u>T</u>hey light_o swimming"

LANGUAGE ARTS ACTIVITY: Proper
Nouns
Answers will vary. Core Words: flash,
where, shine, shine, shock, why

Level 2, Unit 4, Lesson 20
Words with *ch* and *th*

CONTEXT SENTENCES POSTTEST
1. thank   bath
2. peach   thin
3. much   tooth
4. choke   with
5. teach   chick

DICTIONARY ACTIVITY: Example
Sentences
Answers will vary.

HOME-STUDY ENRICHMENT
ACTIVITY
1. much   4. with
2. peach   5. tooth
3. chick, choke

SUPER SPELLERS ACTIVITY

Letter Clues
1. t, h   3. c, h
2. c, h

Definitions
4. pitcher   5. churn

CROSS-CURRICULAR ACTIVITY:
Social Studies

Analogies
1. chief   3. church
2. Earth

Definitions
4. Earth   6. chief
5. church

PROOFREADING ACTIVITY

Misspelled Core Words
1. bath   5. teach
2. choke   6. chick
3. with   7. much
4. tooth   8. thank

Other Corrections
do chicks they warm

LANGUAGE ARTS ACTIVITY:
Pronouns
He, you, She, him, They, them

Level 2, Unit 4, Lesson 21
The /är/ Sound

CONTEXT SENTENCES POSTTEST
1. hard   art
2. yard   park
3. barn   farm
4. shark   sharp
5. cart   dark

DICTIONARY ACTIVITY: Picture
Definitions
Pictures will vary.

HOME-STUDY ENRICHMENT
ACTIVITY

Horizontal: yard, barn, shark, hard, dark

Vertical: sharp, farm, art, park, cart

SUPER SPELLERS ACTIVITY

Phonetic Patterns
1. charming   3. parlor
2. harmless

Base Words
4. harm   6. harmless
5. charm

CROSS-CURRICULAR ACTIVITY:

Phonetic Patterns
1. part   3. carp
2. lark

Classifying
4. carp   6. part
5. lark

Letter Scramble
7. carp   8. part

PROOFREADING ACTIVITY

Misspelled Core Words
1. farm   5. sharp
2. dark   6. barn
3. park   7. yard
4. art   8. cart

Other Corrections
one dark Doing eyes cart

LANGUAGE ARTS ACTIVITY: Verbs
played, changed, bumped, thought
Answers will vary.

Level 2, Unit 4, Lesson 22
The /ûr/ and /or/ Sounds

CONTEXT SENTENCES POSTTEST
1. for   bird
2. horse   more
3. dirt   shirt
4. first   girl
5. horn   short

DICTIONARY ACTIVITY: Example
Sentences
Answers will vary.

HOME-STUDY ENRICHMENT
ACTIVITY

Across	Down
5. horse	1. more
7. girl	2. horn
8. for	3. short
9. shirt	4. first
10. dirt	6. bird

SUPER SPELLERS ACTIVITY

Word Sort
1. explore   3. firm
2. dormitory

Context Clues
4. explore   6. firm
5. dormitory

CROSS-CURRICULAR ACTIVITY:
Science

Phonetic Patterns
1. birch   3. tornado
2. spores

Context Clues
4. birch   6. tornado
5. spores

PROOFREADING ACTIVITY

Misspelled Core Words
1. first   5. for
2. shirt   6. more
3. bird   7. horse
4. dirt   8. horn

Other Corrections
outside dirt "look

LANGUAGE ARTS ACTIVITY:
Adjectives
favorite, beautiful, Happy, first, smart, more, strange, short, kind

Level 2, Unit 4, Lesson 23
Easily Misspelled Words

CONTEXT SENTENCES POSTTEST
1. does   live
2. were   many
3. give   every
4. thing   very
5. who   your

DICTIONARY ACTIVITY: Guide
Words
1. thing   4. give
2. very, were   5. does, every
3. your

HOME-STUDY ENRICHMENT
ACTIVITY
1. does   5. give
2. were   6. live
3. every   7. your
4. very   8. who

SUPER SPELLERS ACTIVITY

Syllables
1. let, skillet   3. tuce, lettuce
2. e, tic, elastic

Riddles
4. lettuce   6. elastic
5. skillet

CROSS-CURRICULAR ACTIVITY:
Social Studies

Phonetic Patterns
1. idea   3. teepee
2. fuel

Letter Scramble
4. fuel   5. teepee

PROOFREADING ACTIVITY

Misspelled Core Words
1. very   5. who
2. live   6. Every
3. Does   7. thing
4. were   8. many

Other Corrections
letter I park The there are jake

LANGUAGE ARTS ACTIVITY: Adverbs
1. loudly; Core Words: Does, your
2. suddenly; Core Words: were, many
3. quietly; Core Word: Every
4. safely; Core Word: thing
5. quickly; Core Word: Who

Level 2, Unit 4, Lesson 24
Review Lessons 19-23

CONTEXT SENTENCES POSTTEST
1. where   peach
2. horse   cart
3. clash   with
4. thing   sharp
5. every   dirt

STANDARDIZED-FORMAT TEST 1
1. a   5. a
2. f   6. k
3. b   7. b
4. h   8. j

PERFORMANCE ASSESSMENT
Students' writings will vary.

STANDARDIZED-FORMAT TEST 2
1. a   5. b
2. h   6. j
3. d   7. a
4. h   8. h

STANDARDIZED-FORMAT TEST 3
1. a   5. a
2. h   6. j
3. c   7. b
4. g   8. f

STANDARDIZED-FORMAT TEST 4
1. a   5. b
2. h   6. f
3. b   7. c
4. h   8. f

STANDARDIZED-FORMAT TEST 5
1. b   5. d
2. f   6. g
3. c   7. c
4. h   8. f

PUZZLE FUN

Across	Down
1. dirt	2. thing
4. every	3. were
6. give	5. your
8. hard	7. where
10. shame	9. does
11. cart	10. sharp
12. park	13. art
14. with	

ANSWER KEY

Level 2, Unit 5, Lesson 25
Words with *br*, *fr*, and *tr*

CONTEXT SENTENCES POSTTEST
1. brag   train
2. trade   frog
3. broom   brick
4. frisky   bright
5. trick   free

DICTIONARY ACTIVITY: Multiple Meanings
1. noun   4. noun
2. verb   5. noun
3. verb   6. noun

HOME-STUDY ENRICHMENT ACTIVITY

Across   **Down**
2. broom   1. bright
4. brag   3. free
7. trade   4. brick
8. frisky   5. train
        6. trick
        8. frog

SUPER SPELLERS ACTIVITY

Letter Clues
1. t, r, trunk   3. b, r, bruise
2. f, r, fracture

Definitions
4. fracture   5. trunk

CROSS-CURRICULAR ACTIVITY:
Science

Word Sort
1. frost   3. trait
2. bran

Word Building
4. bran   6. frost
5. trait

Rhyming Words
7. frost   9. trait
8. bran

PROOFREADING ACTIVITY

Misspelled Core Words
1. bright   5. broom
2. brag   6. train
3. frog   7. frisky
4. brick   8. trade

Other Corrections
fran frog My Fran said

LANGUAGE ARTS ACTIVITY:
Pronoun/Antecedent Agreement
1. He, Rascal
2. It, frog
3. She, Therese
4. They, Christa and George
5. he
6. she

Level 2, Unit 5, Lesson 26
Words with *sl* and *sp*

CONTEXT SENTENCES POSTTEST
1. slip   slick
2. spin   space
3. sled   slide
4. speed   slam
5. speech   spy

DICTIONARY ACTIVITY: ABC order
1. slam   6. space
2. sled   7. speech
3. slick   8. speed
4. slide   9. spin
5. slip   10. spy

HOME-STUDY ENRICHMENT ACTIVITY
1. sled   6. slip
2. speed   7. slide
3. space   8. speech
4. slam   9. spin
5. slick

SUPER SPELLERS ACTIVITY

Word Sort
1. sprain   3. slimy
2. slender

Word Parts
4. sprain   6. slimy
5. slender

CROSS-CURRICULAR ACTIVITY:
Science

Letter Clues
1. s, p   3. s, l
2. s, l

Synonyms
4. spice   6. slime
5. slate

PROOFREADING ACTIVITY

Misspelled Core Words
1. slick   5. speech
2. slip   6. speed
3. space   7. slide
4. spin   8. sled

Other Corrections
the ice slick there is when skaters

LANGUAGE ARTS ACTIVITY:
Subject/Verb Agreement
1. slams   4. spin
2. slip   5. spy
3. slide   6. speeds

Level 2, Unit 5, Lesson 27
Words with *-s*

CONTEXT SENTENCES POSTTEST
1. zebras   animals
2. ants   whales
3. chickens   cows
4. ducks   seals
5. rabbits   snakes

DICTIONARY ACTIVITY: Base Words
1. chicken   5. ant
2. snake   6. seal
3. animal   7. whale
4. zebra   8. cow

HOME-STUDY ENRICHMENT ACTIVITY
Puzzle: animals, ants, chickens, ducks, cows

Letter Scramble
1. seals   3. snakes
2. zebras   4. rabbits

SUPER SPELLERS ACTIVITY

Classifying
1. potatoes   3. boards
2. suspenders

Plurals
4. board   5. potato

Letter Scramble
6. suspenders   8. boards
7. potatoes

CROSS-CURRICULAR ACTIVITY:
Science

Plurals
1. lizard   3. grasshopper
2. ladybug

Context Clues
4. lizards   6. ladybugs
5. grasshoppers

PROOFREADING ACTIVITY

Misspelled Core Words
1. animals   5. snakes
2. ants   6. whales
3. rabbits   7. seals
4. zebras

Other Corrections
animals All food They some animal
Before i

LANGUAGE ARTS ACTIVITY:
Prepositions and Prepositional Phrases
1. for the animals
2. after the ducks
3. before the zebras
4. with the whales
5. under the rabbits
6. on the snakes
7. by the ants
8. from the chickens
9. over the cows

Level 2, Unit 5, Lesson 28
Words that Sound Alike

CONTEXT SENTENCES POSTTEST
1. see   road
2. meet   deer
3. die   dear
4. rode   meat
5. dye   sea

DICTIONARY ACTIVITY: Definitions
1. rode   4. see
2. meet   5. die
3. deer

HOME-STUDY ENRICHMENT ACTIVITY
1. Road, Rode   3. Deer, Dear
2. See, Sea

SUPER SPELLERS ACTIVITY

Homophones
1. bored   3. weigh
2. knew

Letter Clues
4. e, i, g, h, weigh   6. r, e, d, bored
5. k, knew

CROSS-CURRICULAR ACTIVITY:
Social Studies

Homophones
1. cent   3. peak
2. poor

Rhyming Words
4. cent   6. poor
5. peak

PROOFREADING ACTIVITY

Misspelled Core Words
1. rode
2. sea
3. dye
4. road
5. deer
6. die
7. meet

Other Corrections
town, We it seemed suddenly die.

LANGUAGE ARTS ACTIVITY: Verb Tense
1. met, meet
2. see, saw
3. eat, ate

Level 2, Unit 5, Lesson 29
Family Words

CONTEXT SENTENCES POSTTEST
1. mother — father
2. brother — sister
3. baby — family
4. Aunt — Uncle
5. grandmother — grandfather

DICTIONARY ACTIVITY: Base Words
1. aunt
2. father
3. brother
4. grandmother
5. family
6. mother
7. grandfather
8. uncle
9. baby
10. sister

HOME-STUDY ENRICHMENT ACTIVITY
1. mother
2. grandmother
3. sister
4. aunt
5. father
6. grandfather
7. brother
8. uncle
9. baby
10. family

SUPER SPELLERS ACTIVITY

Syllables
1. grand/daugh/ter
2. grand/son
3. grand/pa

Phonetic Patterns
4. grandson
5. granddaughter
6. grandpa

CROSS-CURRICULAR ACTIVITY: Social Studies

Letter Clues
1. ou
2. ie
3. ph

Riddles
4. nephew
5. cousin
6. niece

PROOFREADING ACTIVITY

Misspelled Core Words
1. family
2. mother
3. father
4. grandfather
5. uncle
6. sister
7. aunt
8. baby

Other Corrections
week, food, my grandfather my

LANGUAGE ARTS ACTIVITY: Plurals with -s or -es
1. mothers
2. fathers
3. sisters
4. brothers
5. grandmothers
6. aunts

Level 2, Unit 5, Lesson 30
Review Lessons 25-29

CONTEXT SENTENCES POSTTEST
1. grandmother — snakes
2. speech — sister
3. bright — sea
4. animals — deer
5. train — slip

STANDARDIZED-FORMAT TEST 1
1. e
2. f
3. b
4. g
5. c
6. g
7. d
8. h

PERFORMANCE ASSESSMENT
Students' writings will vary.

STANDARDIZED-FORMAT TEST 2
1. d
2. h
3. b
4. f
5. d
6. h
7. d
8. g

STANDARDIZED-FORMAT TEST 3
1. b
2. h
3. a
4. j
5. c
6. g
7. d
8. f

STANDARDIZED-FORMAT TEST 4
1. a
2. j
3. c
4. g
5. a
6. h
7. b
8. j

STANDARDIZED-FORMAT TEST 5
1. b
2. f
3. c
4. j
5. a
6. h
7. b
8. j

PUZZLE FUN

Across	Down
3. rode	1. speech
4. bright	2. deer
6. train	5. grandmother
9. die	7. frisky
10. animals	8. sea
12. meat	11. snakes
13. baby	
14. sister	
15. slip	

Level 2, Unit 6, Lesson 31
The /ŏŏ/ Sound

CONTEXT SENTENCES POSTTEST
1. book — good
2. push — foot
3. took — hook
4. full — wool
5. pull — bush

DICTIONARY ACTIVITY: Entries
1. 2
2. to move forward with effort
3. I pushed the cart through the market.

HOME-STUDY ENRICHMENT ACTIVITY

Across	Down
2. good	1. wool
4. full	3. push
5. bush	5. book
7. hook	6. foot
8. took	

SUPER SPELLERS ACTIVITY

Phonetic Patterns
1. bookkeeper
2. bookmaker
3. footman

Definitions
4. bookkeeper
5. footman
6. bookmaker

CROSS-CURRICULAR ACTIVITY: Science

Word Building
1. wolf
2. bull
3. wood

Classifying
4. wood
5. wolf
6. bull

PROOFREADING ACTIVITY

Misspelled Core Words
1. took
2. hook
3. wool
4. bush
5. push
6. pull
7. foot
8. full

Other Corrections
my mom i tried away, free, my mom

LANGUAGE ARTS ACTIVITY: Contractions
1. isn't
2. weren't
3. wasn't
4. aren't
5. isn't

Level 2, Unit 6, Lesson 32
Words with -ed or -ing

CONTEXT SENTENCES POSTTEST
1. bat — batting
2. mop — mopped
3. cutting — cut
4. tap — tapped
5. hitting — hit

DICTIONARY ACTIVITY: Entry Words
1. /bat/
2. verb
3. 2

HOME STUDY ENRICHMENT ACTIVITY
1. tap
2. bat
3. mop
4. tapped
5. cutting
6. hitting

SUPER SPELLERS ACTIVITY

Base Words
1. demand
2. print
3. tiptoe

Word Endings
4. demanded
5. tiptoeing
6. printed

CROSS-CURRICULAR ACTIVITY: Social Studies

Word Endings
1. trapped
2. trotted
3. dropped

Classifying
4. trap, trap
5. trot
6. drop, drop

PROOFREADING ACTIVITY

Misspelled Core Words
1. bat
2. batting
3. hit
4. hitting
5. mop
6. mopped
7. tap
8. cutting

ANSWER KEY

Other Corrections
meghan asked͜ ͜"we have ͜"don't

LANGUAGE ARTS ACTIVITY: Endings -ed and -s
1. likes
2. bats
3. hit
4. cleaned
5. like

Level 2, Unit 6, Lesson 33
The /ou/ Sound

CONTEXT SENTENCES POSTTEST
1. sound
2. clown
3. ouch
4. out
5. owl

town
loud
down
house
now

DICTIONARY ACTIVITY: ABC Order
1. down
2. out
3. owl
4. loud
5. now
6. sound
7. house
8. ouch
9. owl
10. clown
11. loud
12. town

HOME STUDY ENRICHMENT ACTIVITY

Context Clues
1. Town
2. Loud
3. Out
4. Clown
5. ouch
6. now
7. owl

SUPER SPELLERS ACTIVITY

Letter Clues
1. o, u, snout
2. o, u, foul
3. o, u, stout

Antonyms
4. foul
5. stout

CROSS-CURRICULAR ACTIVITY: Social Studies

Word Sort
1. route
2. underground railroad
3. tower

Syllables
4. route
5. un/der/ground rail/road
6. tow/er

Rhyming Words
7. route
8. tower

PROOFREADING ACTIVITY

Misspelled Core Words
1. house
2. out
3. town
4. sound
5. owl
6. down
7. clown
8. Now

Other Corrections
i͜ brother͜ i͜ ͜"are

LANGUAGE ARTS ACTIVITY: Pronouns
1. I
2. me
3. I
4. I
5. me

Level 2, Unit 6, Lesson 34
Compound Words

CONTEXT SENTENCES POSTTEST
1. maybe
2. into
3. nobody
4. inside
5. something

notebook
bedroom
lunchroom
doghouse
myself

DICTIONARY ACTIVITY: Example Sentences
Answers will vary.

HOME-STUDY ENRICHMENT ACTIVITY
1. lunchroom
2. notebook
3. doghouse
4. bedroom
5. nobody
6. into

SUPER SPELLERS ACTIVITY

Word Parts
1. spot, light
2. brief, case
3. sun, flower

Context Clues
4. sunflower
5. briefcase
6. spotlight

CROSS-CURRICULAR ACTIVITY: Science

Word Parts
1. thunder, cloud
2. rock, slide
3. land, fill

Word Building
4. rockslide
5. landfill
6. thundercloud

PROOFREADING ACTIVITY

Misspelled Core Words
1. notebook
2. bedroom
3. doghouse
4. nobody
5. myself
6. lunchroom
7. into
8. something

Other Corrections
i͜ left͜ there͜ ͜"don't͜ table͜

LANGUAGE ARTS ACTIVITY: Capitalization
1. Monday; Core Word: bedroom
2. April; Core Word: doghouse
3. Saturday; Core Word: notebook
4. March; Core Word: myself
5. Thursday; Core Word: Nobody
6. Friday; Core Word: lunchroom
7. Sunday; Core Word: Maybe
8. May; Core Word: inside

Level 2, Unit 6, Lesson 35
Number Words

CONTEXT SENTENCES POSTTEST
1. one
2. three
3. five
4. six
5. eight

two
four
ten
seven
nine

DICTIONARY ACTIVITY: Entry Words
1. one
2. 3
3. after
4. Answers will vary.

HOME-STUDY ENRICHMENT ACTIVITY

Across	Down
2. eight	1. nine
4. six	3. two
5. three	4. seven
6. one	5. ten
7. five	7. four

SUPER SPELLERS ACTIVITY

Syllables
1. for/ty
2. sev/en/ty
3. eight/y

Riddles
4. forty
5. seventy
6. eighty

CROSS-CURRICULAR ACTIVITY: Math

Phonetic Patterns
1. ninety
2. fifty
3. thirty

Related Words
4. thirty
5. ninety
6. fifty

PROOFREADING ACTIVITY

Misspelled Core Words
1. one
2. two
3. three
4. four
5. seven
6. eight
7. nine
8. ten

Other Corrections
can͜ first͜ next͜ nine͜

LANGUAGE ARTS ACTIVITY: End Punctuation
1. .; Core Word: four
2. ?; Core Word: nine
3. .; Core Word: three
4. .; Core Word: one
5. !; Core Word: eight
6. ?; Core Word: six

Level 2, Unit 6, Lesson 36
Review Lessons 31-35

CONTEXT SENTENCES POSTTEST
1. cut
2. bat
3. one
4. clown
5. good

foot
out
myself
something
eight

STANDARDIZED-FORMAT TEST 1
1. b
2. f
3. c
4. g
5. e
6. h
7. b
8. f

PERFORMANCE ASSESSMENT
Students' writings will vary.

STANDARDIZED-FORMAT TEST 2
1. b
2. h
3. d
4. h
5. a
6. g
7. d
8. h

STANDARDIZED-FORMAT TEST 3
1. c
2. f
3. d
4. h
5. c
6. f
7. a
8. h

ANSWER KEY

STANDARDIZED-FORMAT TEST 4

1. b
2. f
3. c
4. j

5. a
6. g
7. a
8. h

STANDARDIZED-FORMAT TEST 5

1. d
2. f
3. b
4. h

5. a
6. j
7. c
8. g

PUZZLE FUN

Across

2. clown
5. batting
6. now
8. something
13. mopped
14. full

Down

1. town
2. cut
3. maybe
4. house
7. eight
9. myself
10. ten
11. good
12. foot